P9-CQG-123

DISCIPLINE
THAT
RESTORES

ENDORSEMENTS

This book is a "must read" for teachers, school superintendents and school board members. Ron and Roxanne Claassen provide the expertise of seasoned practitioners, and the theoretical construct of experienced analysts. Through discussion, case scenarios, models, flowcharts, and step by step strategies, they move the reader from vision to "hands on" application in a way that not only engages the mind, but also stretches and stimulates the "heart". I recommend this book to every person seeking to become a more effective leader.

Arthur Wint
Professor of Criminology
Director of Peace and Conflict Studies
Fresno State University

As Roxanne's administrator and a long time educator, I have become a proponent of *Discipline That Restores* (DTR). It is empowering because students, their parents, and community establish mutual respect and learn a constructive way to resolve conflict. Utilizing a punitive system cuts away at the respect and creates a hierarchy of superior and subordinate. DTR establishes mutual respect and accountability. The focus is not on us (educator, administrator, parent) and what we are going to do, the focus is on the student and what they are going to do. The skills acquired through *Discipline That Restores* are life-changing.

Beatriz Ramirez
Superintendent/Principal
Raisin City School District

I believe this book is a major breakthrough in the field of education. Understanding the core issues of getting students to cooperate has never been so clear and concise. *Discipline That Restores* provides classroom teachers with concrete, step by step procedures that enable students to be responsible for their own actions. It empowers teachers to serve their students so that they understand their behavior and take part in the solution. Our student teachers use these strategies to successfully meet the behavioral and learning needs of each student in the classroom. I recommend it to all teachers and especially beginning teachers.

Vickie Bigler
Director of Teacher Education, Visalia Center
Fresno Pacific University

Discipline That Restores presents a compelling vision of restorative discipline, is based on sound theory and research, and is highly practical. While it doesn't use explicitly biblical language, it is consistent with how Jesus interacted with those he encountered. Restorative Discipline transformed the climate of our campuses.

Dr. Jerry Meadows
Superintendent
Immanuel Schools

The models and strategies presented in *Discipline That Restores* transformed our high school campus and opened up communication between students, staff, and parents. School-wide, we implemented classroom respect agreements and conflict resolution strategies. Our previous discipline system did not develop a respectful climate and was unable to help students understand the need to change behavior and resolve conflict. DTR transforms discipline into learning experiences that decrease stress, improve effectiveness, and build relationships.

Ryan Wood
Principal
Immanuel Schools

Discipline That Restores is a welcome addition to the field. Its helpful models and strategies make it a great tool to introduce constructive change in schools. It embodies the essence of restorative justice...living out the principles and values in our daily lives. Ron and Roxanne have been implementing the philosophy of restorative discipline in schools for years and have now put those practical life experiences into words for the rest of us to learn.

Lorraine Stutzman Amstutz
Author: *The Little Book of Restorative Discipline for Schools*

DISCIPLINE
THAT
RESTORES

Strategies to Create Respect,
Cooperation, and Responsibility
In the Classroom

By
Ron and Roxanne Claassen

Foreword
Pamela S. Lane-Garon, Ph.D.

Copyright © 2008 Ron and Roxanne Claassen

Printed in the United States of America.

BookSurge Publishing, South Carolina

International Standard Book Number: 1-4196-9912-1

ISBN-13-9781419699122

Library of Congress Catalog Card Number: 2008907446

All rights reserved.

Permission is hereby given to teachers to make copies of the

Flowchart, Student/Teacher Agreement Form and the Thinkery Form.

Except for brief quotations in critical articles or reviews, no other part of this book may

be reproduced in any manner without permission from Ron or Roxanne Claassen.

First Edition

For information and training contact:
The Center for Peacemaking and Conflict Studies
Fresno Pacific University
1-800-909-8677
pacs@fresno.edu
peace.fresno.edu

To order additional copies of this book visit:
disciplinethatrestores.org
Or
www.booksurge.com

Contents

Chapter 8   Follow-up Meetings   121

Chapter 9   Thinkery   133

Chapter 10   Family Conference   143

Chapter 11 School Authority Structure **153**

Chapter 12 Conclusion: Obstacles and Opportunities **161**

Works Consulted **169**
The Authors **175**

Acknowledgements

We want to start by acknowledging our gratitude to those who have preceded us in developing and writing about theory, models, skills, and strategies in the fields of school discipline, conflict resolution, and restorative justice. We are also grateful to those who have focused their energy and skill on the importance of power and structures.

We want to thank those students and teachers who have taught us so much as they have been willing to "try out" many of the emerging ideas and give us feedback. Many of their ideas and stories are included as examples or illustrations. Some stories are composites, and all names and details have been changed to protect identity.

We want to thank Pamela S. Lane-Garon who wrote the Foreword and who is a tireless advocate for Peer Mediation in our schools.

Roxanne: I want to thank my administrators, who have been encouraging over the years, especially my current administrator Beatriz Ramirez who has been so supportive. I also want to thank Janice Oaxaca and Donna Seward, teachers who drive in a carpool with me each day and are such good listeners. My husband Ron has been the inspiration and encouragement to me to put his very sound, loving, and caring ideas into practice.

Ron: I want to thank Dalton Reimer, who has been co-director with me in the Center for Peacemaking. We have been meeting regularly for over twenty years. Arthur Wint, director of the Peace and Conflict Studies program at Fresno State University, has become a good friend and colleague. Duane Ruth-Heffelbower was there in the early development of the models, questioning and encouraging me. He has also been the Webmaster who has put many of my ideas in a form that makes them accessible to people around the world. The stimulation of the discussions with these and many other friends and colleagues and their encouragement have contributed significantly to this book. Finally, I want to thank my wife Roxanne, who is my best friend and most trusted colleague.

We both want to dedicate this book to our sons, Ryan and Kevin, and their families.

Foreword

Pamela S. Lane-Garon, Ph.D.
California State University, Fresno

Those of us who are involved in the daily work of applying **Conflict Resolution Education (CRE)**, **Peace Education (PE)**, or **Restorative Justice (RJ)** in schools are rejoicing that our combined efforts are gathering momentum around the globe. The book you have begun to read, is, in this professor/practitioner's estimation, a most useful contribution. It is born out of the research and life work of Ron and Roxanne Claassen, who have nurtured the knowledge, skills, and dispositions of conflict resolution, peacemaking, and restorative justice in both their professional and personal lives.

To propose Restorative Discipline or Discipline That Restores (DTR) as described by Ron and Roxanne in public education is indeed courageous. We all know how firmly ideas about traditional school discipline are rooted in notions of punishment and reward. After all, the Puritan Ethic and Skinnerian Behaviorism are part and parcel of our nation's cultural past. Our public schools are perhaps the institutions most illustrative of this heritage. So Ron and Roxanne are brave, but not without foundation. Roxanne's years of work in the Raisin City school system using DTR and Ron's career at Fresno Pacific University where Restorative Discipline now guides university procedures around student behavior are evidence of the model's power and potential to restore.

Discipline That Restores (DTR) is a restorative discipline system for schools, classrooms, and homes that parallels, contributes to, and draws from emerging international conflict resolution education, peace education, and restorative justice movements with emphasis on the last. Before reading further, you may wish to consider the many ways practitioners, educators, and researchers conceptualize their labors in overlapping fields. This understanding may increase your appreciation of the authors' work and message.

Conflict Resolution Education (CRE) curriculum exists for learners in grades kindergarten through graduate school. Some states have wisely integrated this content with language arts, health, and social studies curricula. This book provides an approach for integrating these into the life of the classroom as a community. Teachers teach and children learn that conflict is a natural part of life and that learning constructive conflict-related skills is as important to becoming an educated person as is knowing the order of operations in math. An underlying principle of CRE is that conflict resolution skills are essential for life and should be embraced at all educational levels (Jones, 2004). Said another way, this aspect of social-cognitive human development requires guidance and practice, too. To be prepared for life is to develop knowledge about conflict, confidence in dealing with it, and values around the importance of considering the welfare of all in the conflict-related processes. CRE programs typically fit one of three delivery formats: 1) direct skills instruction, 2) peer mediation, 3) embedded curriculum (Garrard and Lipsey, 2007, p. 12). The book you are about to read focuses classroom CRE on restorative justice practices specific to the relationship between student and teacher.

Peace Education (PE) is an approach inclusive of building knowledge, skills, and disposition to "make peace" and to advocate for the same in a variety of venues. According to UNICEFF (Fountain, 1999):

> Peace education refers to the process of promoting the knowledge,
> skills, attitudes and values needed to bring about behavior changes
> that will enable children, youth and adults to prevent conflict and
> violence, both overt and structural; to resolve conflict peacefully,
> and to create the conditions conducive to peace, whether at an
> intrapersonal, interpersonal, intergroup, national or international
> level.

The international organization, Service Civil International (SCI) defines Peace Education as learning *about* and learning *for* peace:

> Learning *about* peace means obtaining knowledge and understanding
> of what contributes to peace, what damages it, what leads to war,
> what does "peace" mean on each level anyway, what is my role in it,

and how are the different levels connected? Learning *for* peace means learning the skills, attitudes and values that one needs in order to contribute to peace and help maintain it. For example, this means learning to deal with conflicts without the recourse to violence, learning to think creatively, learning to apply the methods of active non violence or learning to deal with cultural differences in a constructive way. (SCI, www.spaceforpeace.net).

While Ron and Roxanne do not emphasize the connection to the peace education movement, their book clearly adds to the knowledge base of educating students to live in community peacefully and responsibly. The book serves as a teacher guide to nurturing knowledge, skills, and disposition to approach conflict constructively. The strategies recommended are both intra and interpersonal. It also guides teachers to create a discipline structure that provides multiple strategies to resolve conflict peacefully.

Restorative Justice (RJ) as defined by Howard Zehr (2002, p. 37) is "a process to involve, to the extent possible, those who have a stake in a specific offense and to collectively identify and address harms, needs, and obligations, in order to heal and put things as right as possible." (Ron is also an international contributor in the RJ movement. In 1996 Ron's Restorative Justice Fundamental Principals were adopted by the United Nations Working Party on Restorative Justice.) Because DTR is firmly rooted in RJ, it is well to consider the RJ goals for change. Again, Howard Zher suggests, "We must have a process that gives attention to those societal needs and obligations that go beyond the ones held by the immediate stakeholders. We also must not lose those qualities which the legal system at its best represents: the rule of law, due process, a deep regard for human rights, the orderly development of law" (2002, p. 60). Schools are very concerned about the latter. The proliferation of "zero tolerance" approaches to educational code violations are evidence of this concern. DTR offers much hope for a sea-change in school climate by providing a strategy that encourages collaboration and cooperation without ignoring due process and the rule of law.

Education has been experimenting with models since the Founding Fathers began to define and advocate for an "American culture." However, in our current essentialist climate—emphasizing accountability and assessment—we now demand evidence-based practices. Knowing *what* to measure and *how* to measure it will also determine the extent to which restorative justice principles find their way into classrooms and whole-school practices (Garrard, 2007). A recent study of schools employing RJ-centered discipline practices in Australia indicates: "for a restorative philosophy to be implemented and sustained in schools, the aspiration must be ... changing from behavior management to relationship management" (Shaw, 2007, p. 134). This is no small task for a system in which behaviorism, with a focus on punishment for negative behavior, reigned for forty years.

Discipline That Restores. Restores what? Respect, order, civility, face, accountability, integrity, dignity, hope? If you are an administrator, teacher, or counselor, as you read this book, you may find yourself envisioning an approach to discipline in the schools that looks, sounds, and feels very different from what you or your children experienced. Read on!

Introduction: Why *Discipline That Restores?*

It has been said that 10% of your life experience is dependent on what happens to you and 90% is based on how you respond. While this may seem like an exaggeration, the saying certainly emphasizes the importance of how we respond, especially when faced with conflict or misbehavior.

Every teacher responds in some way when a conflict arises. Often the response is unconscious, based on a habit or pattern that is quite predictable. These patterns are often the ones we learned in our early life. Sometimes, when we are fortunate, these patterns are helpful and constructive, but often they are not. The good news is that due to increased study and experience in the areas of conflict resolution and restorative justice, strategies are emerging that teachers can utilize to respond in ways that are more effective, constructive, and life-giving than the punishment habits that only result in short-term behavior change and long term resentment and rebellion.

Roxanne Claassen has been implementing these ideas throughout her career, primarily as an eighth-grade teacher. Over the years, fellow teachers and administrators would ask her what she was doing in her classroom that made it such a lively yet orderly and safe place, where students actually valued conflict resolution and problem solving. Roxanne's colleagues wanted to know how to duplicate what she was doing in her classroom, and even how this could be implemented school-wide.

After many requests from teachers and administrators, we have written this book to make the models, skills, strategies, and structures to implement what we call Discipline That Restores (DTR) accessible to anyone who might find it useful. This book contains the experience and insights we have gathered over the last thirty years. It contains many stories and illustrations of real experiences about real students (names and some details have been changed to protect student identities).

We believe that any teacher who wants to can implement the DTR Flowchart. Many teachers have told us that using the DTR structure reduces their stress, since they now have a plan for responding to any conflicts they encounter. They often say, as

Roxanne says, that discipline has become one of their favorite parts of teaching. They also have found that they waste less time and energy in ineffective power struggles with students. DTR helps teachers create a structure that is life-giving and constructive for the teacher and *all* students (not just the "good" students).

Many teachers leave the teaching profession due to high stress related to attempting to control students. A basic question all teachers must ask is whether they are going to control students through fear of punishment (which adds stress) or by creating a cooperative community based on the development and maintenance of *right relationships* (which decreases stress). The research demonstrates that when administrators and teachers use the models within this book to respond to conflict and misbehavior, the likelihood of using a cooperative process, having a constructive outcome, and being a more effective leader increases significantly. DTR theory, skills, and strategies help create a safe and cooperative setting in which students are able to learn and teachers have more time and energy to teach.

Background

The two of us, Ron and Roxanne, have been married for forty years. Our friendship has grown with each passing year. Our success as a couple has not been because we never had conflicts. Like all couples and families (we have two grown sons who are both married), we have our share of conflicts. We would say our relationship has grown because of the way we have resolved the conflicts.

For example, when our sons were about five and seven, we decided we would set aside each Friday night for family fun night. But it was not long before we were spending a good portion of the evening arguing about what constituted "fun." We finally had a family meeting to talk about it. What emerged was an agreement to take turns planning our fun evenings (an adult helping each child, when it was his turn, to help stay within the budget). We agreed to allow the person to decide where we would eat, what we would do, what music we would listen to as we drove, who would sit where in the car (except that they could not drive until they had legal permits), etc. At the end of the evening we would all compliment the planner on something we enjoyed during the evening. We would not complain or try to influence his or her decisions (this was a challenge for all of us). We decided to try it for eight weeks and then reevaluate. At the end of eight weeks we decided that we wanted to continue. We made adjustments as our sons grew up. Now that they have left home, the two of us still use this plan. What started with a conflict grew into something that was effective and life-giving, and it improved our relationships. We think every conflict has that potential.

Ron's major contributions to this book are the Flowchart, models, and strategies that embody the theory of restorative justice and the best practices of conflict resolution. Ron acknowledges many before him and his contemporaries who contributed to these fields and laid a solid foundation on which to build. Many of their works are listed in the Works Consulted.

Ron's unique entry into the fields of conflict resolution and restorative justice, from the background of studying (Master of Arts degree, 1968) and teaching mathematics (1968–1978), contributed to his diligent observation of patterns and his devotion to creating models and strategies. In 1982, after completing a Master of Divinity degree with an emphasis in counseling, Ron founded and directed the Victim Offender Reconciliation Program (VORP) in Fresno, California (the first in California). He also developed a private mediation practice. In 1990, Ron was invited to join the faculty at Fresno Pacific College (now University) as the cofounder and codirector of the Center for Peacemaking and Conflict Studies. The Peacemaking Model, which emerged from observing victims and offenders reconcile, describes how people who are angry or upset due to experiences of violation can move to where things are okay or even good between them.

Having observed the criminal justice system, with its focus on violation of law and the use of punishment, and its contrast with the emerging ideas of restorative justice, Ron developed the DTR Principles to reflect how Roxanne was implementing restorative justice in her classroom. Later Ron developed a series of principles (initially for the local VORP, adopted by the UN Working Party on Restorative Justice, 1996; see peace.fresno.edu/docs/rjprinc.html) that describe restorative justice as a way of working with violations that focuses justice on "making things as right as possible" rather than on punishment.

Ron also developed the Four Options Model to describe the basic ways people deal with conflict, defined as "power, rights, and interests" by Ury, Brett, and Goldberg of the Harvard Negotiation Project. In model form, it became the four, rather than three, basic ways people deal with conflict. This model was the focus of Ron's doctoral dissertation completed in 2005. While these models have broad applications, this book applies them to the work of teachers and schools. Ron has been consulting with and training administrators and teachers for over twenty years.

After our two sons were well along in school and after helping start VORP (1982–1986), Roxanne completed her teaching credential (including an additional major in conflict and peacemaking) and began teaching at Raisin City School. Her teaching experience included first, fourth, fifth, sixth, and eighth (for the last eleven years) grades. When she started teaching, after having helped start the Victim Offender Reconciliation Program in Fresno, she was surprised to find that the way misbehavior is handled in schools is very similar to the way the criminal justice system handles it. The two of us began thinking together about how discipline in school could incorporate the skills and strategies that were emerging in the fields of conflict resolution/mediation and restorative justice—in particular, the models that Ron had been developing.

Roxanne noticed that while our schools have a well-developed academic curriculum, the social curriculum receives less attention in teacher training and at the school and state levels. Due to the underlying punishment paradigm, it seems to duplicate what teachers and administrators experienced when they were students. As Jane Nelsen points out, it assumes the myth that the best way to get students to act better is to punish them for misbehavior. This paradigm is rarely examined. In fact, punishment structures are so embedded in our way of thinking that they usually just happen without anyone giving them a great deal of thought and attention. Roxanne observed that our responses to conflict or misbehavior are part of the social curriculum and could be the occasion for adults and students to connect constructively at the deepest levels. She observed that the approach used by adults at schools had tremendous influence on relationships. Some responses stigmatized or ostracized students and damaged teacher/student relationships, while others restored and reintegrated students and improved teacher/student relationships.

Roxanne completed her Master of Arts in Peacemaking and Conflict Studies in 2003. One of her projects was developed into *Making Things Right*, a thirty-two-lesson curriculum (see disciplinethatrestores.org/) for training students to be constructive conflict resolvers and mediators. Her thesis reflected on her journey in the development of DTR and contributed to its ongoing progress. Roxanne has been working at implementing restorative justice/discipline principles in her classroom for the last seventeen years. She has taught at a variety of grade levels including first, fourth, fifth. sixth, seventh, and eighth grades (both departmentalized, and self-contained).

Roxanne believes that almost any discipline program can work reasonably well for eighty to ninety percent of students in a classroom, since most students are respectful, cooperative, and rarely involved in the formal discipline structure. The particularly compelling thing about DTR is that it also works very well with students who arrive with a reputation, are the least cooperative, and give teachers problems over and over again. Roxanne has found that DTR works with students who are on the fringes of despair, deciding whether they want to be a part of the community or join a counter-community that is not connected with the academic world of the other students. Roxanne is not saying that this is easily accomplished. The teacher must be very committed to continuing to work with such students because the DTR plan does not give up on anyone. DTR provides many levels of effective backup strategies for a student who is temporarily uncooperative. Roxanne finds this approach energizing and less stressful than the alternatives.

Students observe their teachers and learn not just from what they say, but also from what they do. Learning, especially for the social curriculum, is so much more than what teachers write down in the lesson plan books, even after careful consideration of each standard that the state has identified must be met. Roxanne observed that students are much more likely to pick up on what she does and how she acts than on what she says. If there is a discrepancy between what she is doing and what she is saying, students tend to believe what she is doing. For example, if she says that it is best to resolve conflict cooperatively but then she uses coercion to handle a conflict between her and the students, they know that what she really values is the ability to use coercion. The teacher wants to be sure she is doing what leads to responses of increased understanding and love. Noting that the word *disciple* and *discipline* are closely related, both stemming from the Latin word for student, Roxanne realized that in one sense, her students are her disciples. Accepting this tremendous responsibility, she has decided that she wants what they learn from being with her to be constructive, life-giving, and to contribute to improved relationships.

DTR Theory

While this is primarily a "how-to" book, it is deeply rooted in theory and research. While a thorough discussion of the theory is beyond the scope of this book, the comments below provide an introduction.

The theory of restorative justice (Zehr, Pranis, Van Ness, Umbreit, Bazemore, McElrea, Wright, Claassen, and others) points the way to a new paradigm and the development of what could be done in a well-planned social curriculum in a school. Using the insights of restorative justice and conflict resolution theory, applying the skills and strategies developed by Ron, and reflecting constantly on the resulting impact has led to the development of the DTR Flowchart and the step-by-step plan that we present in this book. Roxanne's master's thesis describes the pedagogy (Gordon, Glasser, Freire, Ginott, Nelsen) needed to encourage better behavior and improved relationships while valuing individual responsibility and community accountability.

As Roxanne noticed when she started teaching, school discipline systems often look a lot like the criminal justice system. They focus on what rule was violated, who violated the rule, and what should be done to punish the wrongdoers (make them feel worse in hopes they will act better), just as the criminal justice system focuses on answering three basic questions: What law was violated? Who violated the law? And what is the appropriate punishment for the lawbreaker? All decisions are made by the responsible authorities. All of this is done in hopes that the offender will change behavior in the future due to the fear of or unpleasantness of the punishment. But this is only one way of viewing justice.

Restorative justice provides another paradigm focused on responsibility, accountability, and a goal of restoration for all impacted by the offense. Restorative justice asks a different set of questions: Who was harmed? What are the needs of the harmed? How can things be made as right as possible? and How can things be changed to create a better future? A restorative justice system prefers that the decisions are made in a cooperative process by all of the impacted parties rather than just the authorities. If impacted people are not willing, or they try and can't find agreement, then the authorities seek ways to address the same questions. DTR is a restorative justice discipline system for schools, classrooms, and homes that parallels, contributes to, and draws from the emerging international restorative justice movement.

In 1996, Ron drafted a set of principles for restorative justice that were adopted by the United Nations NGO Working Party on Restorative Justice as their starting point in preparing for the 2000 UN Crime Congress (see peace.fresno.edu/docs/rjprinc. html).

Ron based these Restorative Justice Principles on the DTR Principles he had written several years earlier. The DTR Principles were written initially to describe what

Roxanne was doing in her classroom, which was based on combined knowledge and experience with VORP, our studies in peacemaking and conflict resolution, and our experience as teachers. The DTR Principles served as a guide, or a "rudder" for testing emerging ideas, strategies, and practices. Implementing the theory expressed in the DTR Principles eventually led to the creation of the DTR Flow Chart.

Below is an overview of the principles. If you are interested in seeing a fuller explanation of these principles, which provide the underlying theory behind this book, you can read an article at disciplinethatrestores.org/IntroDTR.pdf.

Overview of DTR Principles

Purpose: The purpose of DTR is to guide teachers to respond to each conflict or misbehavior in ways that are life-giving and make things as right as possible. DTR uses each conflict and misbehavior to help students learn respect, critical thinking, and cooperative negotiation skills. DTR responses recognize and respect individual freedom while improving relationships and building community life in the classroom.

Problem: DTR recognizes that rules are written to create and protect safety and fairness. DTR also recognizes that when a rule is violated, it points to the real problem. The real problem is not the rule violation but the violation of a person and/or the damage to their property.

People: DTR prefers that the response to the conflict or misbehavior be between the ones who were impacted by the offense. This means that DTR would prefer that when a student is disrespectful with a teacher, the student and teacher should be the primary parties involved in deciding what should be done to make things as right as possible.

Process: DTR prefers that the process used to determine how to make things right include recognizing the violation/conflict, searching for agreements to restore equity and to clarify the future, and following up on the agreements. DTR recognizes that trust grows when agreements are made and kept. That is why it is so important for the primary parties between whom the violation/conflict occurred be involved in the process of making agreements to make things as right as possible.

Power: DTR prefers "power with" to "power over." "Power with" is the kind of power where the teacher and student agree only to those ways of making things right that are life-giving, effective, and improve relationships. This does not mean that the teacher does not ever use "power over," but it does mean that the teacher uses "power over" only in ways that are reasonable, respectful, restorative and intended to reintegrate the misbehaving student, and only when the student is not willing to cooperate.

Overview of the Chapters

Each chapter in the book is focused on what we are calling a "stop" on the DTR Flowchart. You will note that each chapter begins with a copy of the DTR Flowchart and bold arrows from the chapter title to the stop on the Flowchart. We also sometimes refer to the Flowchart as a map. Each chapter includes the purpose of the stop on the Flowchart, the skill needed to implement it, a brief reference to the theory behind it, and an example or story to illustrate the stop. The detail, at most stops, includes some possible language or script a teacher might use to implement it.

It is common to describe a class by dividing it into three parts: 80% who are generally cooperative and on task; 15% who need some additional training and support to be cooperative and on task; and 5% who are very difficult and need a lot of training and support to be cooperative and on task. (See this Web page, which describes the research for positive behavioral support: www.coe.missouri.edu/~rpdc/ howPBSworks. html.)

Using these categories, all of the students benefit from Chapter 1: Teacher Preparation; Chapter 2: Understanding Student/Teacher Conflict; Chapter 3: Usual Constructive Reminders; and Chapter 4: Respect Agreement. The models, skills, and strategies in these chapters address almost all of the issues in the 80% category and many in the 15% and 5% categories. Chapter 5: Active Listening and/or I-Messages (active listening and I-message skills are used at all stops and specifically at this stop) and Chapter 6: Four Options Model are useful with all students but are more frequently needed with the 15% and the 5%. Chapter7: Student/Teacher Meeting, Chapter 8: Follow-up Meeting(s), and Chapter 9: Thinkery are rarely used with the 80%, less frequently utilized with the 15%, and most often used with the 5%. Chapter 10: Family Conference is utilized almost exclusively with the 5%, and Chapter 11: School Authority Structure is utilized with the 5% if needed at all. There are many academic years when Roxanne does not need the School Authority Structure at all.

The two of us have collaborated on the entire book but as you will note, Roxanne has taken the lead on some of the chapters and Ron on others. Roxanne's contribution is primarily on the implementation in the classroom and Ron's in the construction of the Flowchart and models and the development of skills and strategies. Please note along the way that there are a number of references to Website addresses that contain articles written by Roxanne or Ron that further describe some ideas that we decided were beyond the scope of this book.

Students have the resources within them to meet many of the needs that are created when students have conflicts with each other. Student/student mediation programs provide the structure they need to help each other. These programs have proven to improve school climate and safety. We think that these mediation programs for students are very important, but we have chosen not to address them in this book. Also, we think that staff members should have respect agreements and plans to address conflicts. This also is important, but we have decided to leave that to some other book or articles. Finally, while we include a brief chapter on the School Authority Structure in the context of it being a backup for the teacher's discipline system, we are leaving a more thorough development of it to another book or article.

Ron was actively involved in the development of the Restorative Discipline Policy at Fresno Pacific University. Since the time the structure was changed to allow all cases to have a Community Justice Conference (a type of mediation or circle, depending on the situation), only one case each year has needed the School Authority Structure for a final decision. All others were resolved in the context of the Community Justice Conference and the follow-up meetings. One of our resident directors who was most reluctant when the new policy was introduced now says that in addition to addressing each issue that comes up at a deeper and more lasting level, his relationship with the student always improves, which is in sharp contrast to when he was responsible for carrying out the punitive model. The Policy Document can be found at www.fresno.edu/sharedmedia/studentlife/restorativediscipline.pdf, and an article describing the development and early implementation of the policy can be found at http://disciplinethatrestores.org/

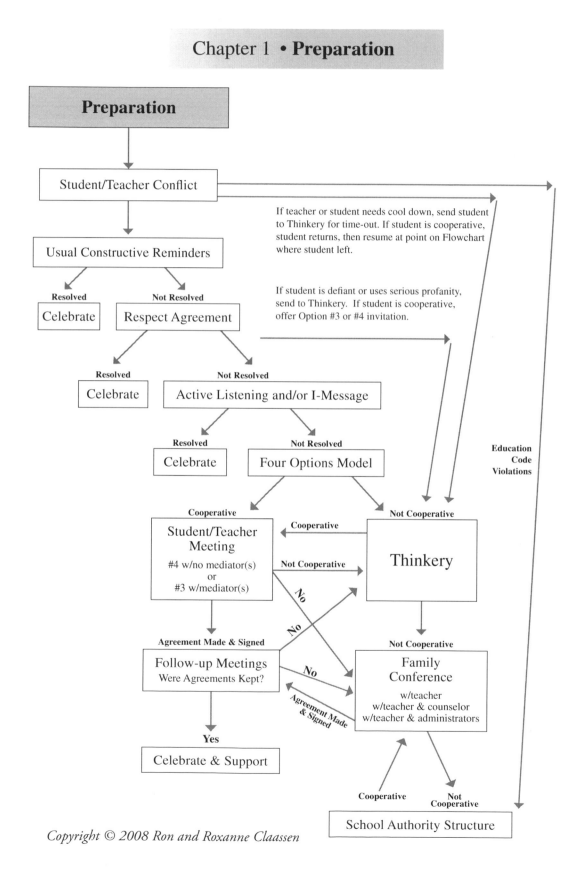

Chapter 1 • **Preparation**

Preparation

Student/Teacher Conflict

If teacher or student needs cool down, send student to Thinkery for time-out. If student is cooperative, student returns, then resume at point on Flowchart where student left.

Usual Constructive Reminders

If student is defiant or uses serious profanity, send to Thinkery. If student is cooperative, offer Option #3 or #4 invitation.

Resolved
Celebrate

Not Resolved
Respect Agreement

Resolved
Celebrate

Not Resolved
Active Listening and/or I-Message

Resolved
Celebrate

Not Resolved
Four Options Model

Education Code Violations

Cooperative
Student/Teacher Meeting
#4 w/no mediator(s)
or
#3 w/mediator(s)

Cooperative

Not Cooperative
Thinkery

Not Cooperative

Not Cooperative

No

No

No

Agreement Made & Signed
Follow-up Meetings
Were Agreements Kept?

Agreement Made & Signed

Not Cooperative
Family Conference
w/teacher
w/teacher & counselor
w/teacher & administrators

Yes
Celebrate & Support

Cooperative

Not Cooperative

School Authority Structure

Copyright © 2008 Ron and Roxanne Claassen

Chapter 1
Preparation

Introduction

The first stop on the DTR Flowchart is preparation. Preparation related to discipline is of utmost importance. When parents send their precious children to school, they want them to be treated with respect and kindness. Parents trust teachers with their most important creation, their children. They know that their children need guidance. They know that their children can behave in ways that need correction. They have no problem with that idea. What they do have a problem with is correction being done in a way that makes their children feel worse about themselves and about learning, rather than better. The best way to ensure a constructive response to misbehavior is to have our social curriculum as well planned as our academic curriculum.

All of our schools have discipline plans. A dictionary definition describes discipline as teaching and instruction. This teaching is to include training that corrects, molds, or perfects the mental faculties or moral character of the student. Added to this is the notion that discipline is orderly or prescribed conduct. It is self-control. It is a rule or system of rules governing conduct or activity. A teacher is in the classroom to do all of this and more. This is a high calling. When it comes to the idea of discipline, teachers must decide how they are going to do it in a way that promotes the most learning while preserving the dignity of each student. We have discovered this to be most possible when we stop focusing on control and put more effort into building community.

A Vision for a Peaceful, Fair, and Effective Classroom

A vision is an administrator's and teacher's hope and guide. A vision is something that doesn't yet exist and is currently seen only in our imagination. It is rooted in values, spirit, and ideals. In our imagination, we see images of classrooms, students, teachers, programs, interactions, and procedures that incorporate these values and ideals. A vision is a desired state for the future. It is more intuitive than linear thinking.

When we think of a vision or a visionary, we may think of something or someone utopian, something that doesn't exist, or someone who may be considered a bit (or a lot) out of touch with reality. But we are going to suggest that a vision is actually very practical.

Teachers and schools that don't have vision will likely find themselves floundering or flitting from here to there, or getting stuck in a rut. Vision gives us freedom to wander about, experiment, and make changes with less fear or threat. We can do this because we test our changes against our vision. Is the change moving us in the direction of our vision?

Our visual image of our vision changes as we gain new insights and as reality around us changes. Yet the core values do not change. Restorative justice and peacemaking are core values in our vision, but our visual images change as we gain new insights through study and life experience.

Vision is more than just a dream. It is that image of our desired state of affairs that reaches all the way back to our current action. It is vision that motivates us to do something, and it is that same vision that guides us along the way.

Our vision for restorative discipline and peacemaking is rooted in peace-*shalom* as described in the Hebrew and Christian texts. One of the hallmarks of peace-*shalom* is an absence of the fear of being harmed.

We love to imagine or envision a world, a community, a school, a classroom, or even a family in which all people experience no fear of being harmed. It does not suggest to us that there will be no conflict, but that in the midst of the conflict the participants do not need to be afraid. Each would know that the other's intention is constructive. Everyone could feel safe, and the only question would be how to transform the conflict or violation into a just and peaceful way for everyone. This kind of peace is an incredible thought. We might even say it is almost unimaginable!

The vision that guides and permeates this book is that schools and classrooms can become places where administrators, teachers, and students are equipped with models, skills, structures, and strategies so that when conflict emerges, they can envision peace-*shalom* and confidently put a constructive process into action. The Flowchart provides a visual description of a sequenced series of skills and strategies, which, when implemented, increase the likelihood of moving in the direction of this vision.

We have divided Preparation on the Flowchart into three parts: teacher preparation, student preparation, and preparing to work constructively with parents. Roxanne will be describing her thoughts and experiences for this first stop on the DTR Flowchart.

Teacher Preparation

Roxanne: I start the process of community building by making conscious decisions about how I want to respond to students. A good time to work at this is during time off or when one is in the preparation stages of welcoming a new class. However, this decision can be made any time one becomes aware of the need for it. I especially want to be aware of how I respond to students at times of stress and misbehavior. Whether it is conscious or not, some decision will be made and implemented. I want to be very aware of what that decision will be. I do not want it to simply happen—sometimes we excuse what we do as being something we just couldn't help, it just happened before we could think about it. When a way of responding simply happens, I have found my response is often not as restorative as one that is made with thought and deliberation. We must become aware of the decision we're making in order to move toward restoration.

A valued friend, who is a pastor, spoke about children and teaching. She put forth the idea that children need love the most when they deserve it the least. This spoke to me as a teacher. Perhaps all of us need love the most when we deserve it the least. Thinking about this idea helps to focus what I want to do as a teacher before I enter the classroom. It is a way for me to prepare to love (*agape*) each of my students.

Ron likes to use the Greek word *agape* to describe love. In the Greek, there are three words that get translated into our English word, *love. Eros* is for romantic love. *Philia* is for brotherly and sisterly love. *Agape* is love given whether or not it is returned. Ron describes that kind of love as a commitment to be constructive. Being constructive means being patient, kind, and self-controlled, and looking for "our" way rather than insisting on my way. This is similar to what Fisher and Brown describe as an unconditionally constructive strategy in their book, *Getting Together: Building Relationships as We Negotiate.* Fisher and Brown say that an unconditionally constructive strategy requires that I work at understanding by balancing reason with emotion, by working at good communication, by being reliable, by using persuasion rather than coercion, and by working at acceptance. Thinking about this, and making a commitment to do it, heads me in the direction of being able to have a restorative response to my students (giving them *agape* when they least deserve it). We are in a human relationship with each other. Misbehavior by either of us damages our relationship. But I, as the adult, can make a decision about my response that can open the door to repairing that relationship.

Without making this conscious decision, I would not be able to respond constructively to situations such as Victor calling the girls "sluts" and otherwise harassing them; Judy flirting with the known boyfriend of Sandy, causing Sandy to tell all the other girls to stop showing Judy any friendship whatsoever; Juan running up close to people and acting like he is going to karate chop them or kick them instead of getting to work on an assignment; Tom launching into a show that disrupts the flow of the class the minute you start introducing a new concept that must be learned; or Stephen muttering a profanity under his breath that you know is directed at you. It is hard to respond out of *agape*, an unconditionally constructive strategy, if you have not committed yourself to this response ahead of time.

Luckily, children are understanding and forgiving. They allow you to correct your response when you stop to think and get it where you want it to be—a response that respects the student and lets them know the behavior is something that needs to change. Actually these students, whom one would describe as misbehaving, are giving you the gift of letting you know that this is a learning opportunity. We learn best from those with whom we have a good relationship. Restorative discipline focuses on the relationship of those directly involved in a conflict. This is a teachable moment. This is about how we live in a community with one another. This is about civility. These are standards all of us are mandated to teach.

Getting in touch with one's values can be another aspect of preparation that is helpful and beneficial. I think about the things I value in relationships. These things include respect, caring, kindness, patience, sharing, self-control, fairness, justice, etc. I want to let students know explicitly what I value. I believe it is how we are in relationships with others that makes what we value become the most apparent. We model our values constantly in how we speak to others and in how we treat them.

One intriguing idea that has shaped my "beginning of the year" plan is that of things being upside down. D.B. Kraybill describes this idea in his book, *The Upside-Down Kingdom*. The idea is related to a new way of thinking about people and structures that will be upside down in sharp relief against the prevailing hierarchical social landscape. This new social structure invites me to do things differently. For example, the prevailing social structure says that if children are to be considered respectful, they should do that which adults tell them to do, and they should do it immediately. This is "power over." What I have found to be more helpful is to be willing and open to discuss with children what needs to be done and how it might be accomplished. We can come to an agreement together. The things that need to be done still get done. The difference is that the students experience this as "power with" rather than "power over." This time of needing to solve a problem is also often the place where real teaching, learning, and improving relationships occurs (often I am one of the learners). Many perceive this as being upside down, and even wrong. It goes against their idea of how the social order should be. This upside-down social order calls on me to value children as much as I value adults. It calls on me to value the student who is misbehaving as much as the one who is cooperating. These values are driven by a choice, not just by doing what comes naturally.

A child who is misbehaving (not cooperating) does not need to hear, "Get out of my class." Usually that is the time they really need an extension of love (*agape*) and concern (another example of things being turned upside down). I am not saying we ignore the misbehavior. We need to pay a great deal of attention to that. The other thing we must pay attention to, however, is the person. It is so important to let the person know you continue to like/love them. However, it is very hard for a child who is being told to leave the room to believe this. What you do not like is whatever it is they are doing that is causing the problem—the focus needs to be on the problem, not just the person. In these situations I find it helpful to think about what I would prefer and what I know to be right. Based on my values, I prefer a structure without punishment at the center, a structure that seeks to restore each person in a spirit of gentleness—gentleness toward the person and an expectation of change toward the behavior. A discipline experience within the DTR structure often takes more effort and is more difficult for a student than to be punished, because DTR invites accepting responsibility and expects new behavior rather than taking one's punishment with no need or promise to change.

It has been important to commit myself to being constructive when I am confronted with a conflict, misbehavior, or a problem with a student or students. Where do I start with such a commitment? I use a scale developed by Ron called Contrasting and Cooperative Values (see disciplinethatrestores.org). The scale takes the ideas of love (defined in this context as a willingness to be constructive) and contrasts them with not-love (defined in this context as acting in a non-cooperative manner). Using the scale, I ask myself if I am willing to be patient, kind, courteous, self-controlled, accepting, seeking our way, etc., in working at our problems and differences. When I can answer yes to this, I know I am ready to work at being constructive when conflicts arise.

Throughout the year, I listen for encouragement in this undertaking during both formal and informal conversations. An idea that spoke to me had to do with asking myself if I am looking for self-protection or self-offering (this was in the context of extending love to enemies). Sometimes we need to do both. So much of DTR has to do with balance. Using the idea of telling a student to leave the classroom, I can show what I mean by balance. There are occasions when it is helpful for both the teacher and the student to have a little separation. This is the self-protection part. However, one must have a plan in place for how that student will leave the room and for what will happen when that student returns. The student may need to leave the room so the teacher and the class can experience self-preservation (students deserve to be able to learn free from disruption). Before the student is asked to leave, he or she should be offered each invitation to cooperate from the Flowchart (Usual Reminders, Respect Agreement, I-Message/Active Listening, Four Options). In the case of my school, leaving the classroom means going to a place to think with an adult who is present to help that process (Thinkery, Chapter 9). The purpose of this is to prepare that student to return to class ready to set up a time to meet with the teacher. This meeting between the teacher and the student becomes the place for self-offering (Student/ Teacher Meeting, Chapter 7).

I do not think it is good to simply ignore the student and the problem upon their return, hoping for self-protection. We sometimes hope it is possible to send students someplace else to be fixed. This is rare. In fact, the student often finds the place to which they are sent to be quite interesting, and the people there often wonder why one could be so upset with such a nice child (so much for self-preservation). The reverse of this happens when there is self-offering and you do not simply ignore the student, hoping that being sent out of the room will have corrected the behavior. If you and that student can come to some understandings and agreements, you gain more self-protection and so do they. You reduce the chance that this will happen over and over again. Many teachers finally turn to side-by-side problem solving when they realize they have given the same child ten detentions for the same thing and the behavior is getting worse rather than better. (A formal Student/Teacher Meeting will be discussed in detail in Chapter 7.)

I want to briefly describe what I commit myself to in my preparation for each new class. I make a commitment to work directly and constructively with all students and especially with any student with whom I have a conflict. I commit myself to using the DTR Flowchart, which maps a constructive strategy of ever-increasing intensity (constructive escalation) to keep inviting the uncooperative student to become cooperative. I commit to meeting with students for whom usual reminders, the respect agreement, and active listening/I-messages do not gain their cooperation. If that meeting does not result in resolution, I don't give up. Following the Flowchart, I schedule a Family Conference (Chapter 10). I ask for parent input as we continue to try to resolve our conflict together. If that does not work, I still do not give up! I enlarge the group by inviting parent/s, other close relatives the immediate family thinks would be helpful, and the school administration to join us to help us solve the problem. This usually gets the problem resolved. It takes some time and effort, but I've found I only need to do this with one or two students per school year. And, it benefits the student and the teacher—and the rest of the class, for that matter—so much that it is well worth it.

I must share here that there have been two situations in the last sixteen years where the group, which included student, parents, administration, and me, has concluded together that the student would voluntarily seek to enter another school. The meetings made it clear that the student and their parents did not choose to do the things required to solve the problem, so everyone was able to say this was a good resolution even though it did not feel great. But it was better than our school making the student leave involuntarily. In another way it was a good resolution because that student's choosing to leave was a benefit to the rest of the class. Still, I would have preferred that the student would have decided to cooperate.

Through making these beginning-of-the-year commitments and practicing them, I have learned that what I do is far more important than what I say. Modeling is a very compelling teaching method. I find that students imitate the ways in which they have been treated. I must, as their teacher, make the decision to model what I say. I want to be a reflector of the ideals for which I want them to aim—I want to model a forgiving and a reconciling spirit. I want my life and the way I act to demonstrate the values I hold related to peace, love, acceptance, justice, and reconciliation. Time spent in reflection and making decisions before I enter the classroom ensures that what I do when I am with my students will be restorative.

Student Preparation

Roxanne: Student preparation is an integral part of the DTR process. Getting things started in a positive direction is enhanced by giving students the assignment of writing about their learning goals for the year. These can then become a part of the second step on the DTR Flowchart—what is called Usual Reminders (Chapter 2).

Having students write about their goals is also a part of my preparation as a teacher because I must become well acquainted with my students very quickly to get the academic program off and running. I have found student goal-writing to be helpful in the process of getting acquainted (in addition to goals, I learn a lot about their writing skills) and forming community. Students find it helpful to realize that they do have some high standards for themselves. It gets the picture in their heads tuned into some pretty incredible goals they have for success at school. It is so encouraging to read those precious papers and discover that there is not one student sitting in the classroom who does not want academic success no matter what their dress, posture, or outward actions might say. Although they don't write this, I have found that they all want to be loved, encouraged, and appreciated. (Eighth graders are actually like very large first graders who say, "Watch me, watch me!") High stakes testing has caused all of us to focus on achievement. I find that the students' written goals are very much in keeping with what the state requires. No student has ever stated that he or she wants less than to be "on grade level." What an exciting and challenging place to start a new school year!

I begin preparing them to write their goals by sharing with them that I have spent time establishing my own goals and making decisions. I take this opportunity to let my students know the tone I want to set for discipline and problem solving. It is important to share my decisions and ideas for classroom structure with my students. Telling them my goals helps me work toward accomplishing those goals, because it gives me an accountability group. I know their goals will help them in the same way.

I always read *Teacher and Child*, by Dr. Hiam Ginott, to my students.

> I have come to a frightening conclusion. I am the decisive element
> in the classroom. It is my personal approach that creates the climate.

It is my daily mood that makes the weather. As a teacher, I possess tremendous power to make a child's life miserable or joyous. I can be a tool of torture or an instrument of inspiration. I can humiliate or humor, hurt or heal. In all situations, it is my response that decides whether a crisis will be escalated or de-escalated, and a child humanized or dehumanized.

I inform them of my commitment/goal to be on the positive end of the spectrum the Ginott passage identifies. I tell my class I plan to be constructive with them in the conflict situations that arise. This means that I plan to not react, but to control my behavior. I want to listen to their concerns. I prefer to do side-by-side problem solving. I let them know I will be teaching them problem-solving skills and a structure that will be used by the class to solve problems.

I inform them that part of problem solving is getting to know ourselves. I invite them to think about some of their goals for the school year. I give them each paper for reflecting on this. I ask them to be very specific about what they want to accomplish this year at school. They are encouraged to think about academic goals such as: What reading level do you want to reach? What would you need to do to reach that level? What do you want to accomplish in math? What would you need to do to accomplish that? What about science, writing, social studies, and art or music? They are also encouraged to think about their goals beyond the academic: What other things do you want to do at school? Are you interested in sports, yearbook, mediation, field trips, science projects, tutoring, etc.? I let them know I will be reading their goals, keeping them and meeting with them from time to time to review them to see how they are going.

As stated earlier, I have never had a student who has not had some positive goals. Some of them have much better strategies in mind for accomplishing their goals, and this is something that can be learned. We work at learning this directly, often when we meet to problem solve. I get out the goals of the student with whom I am meeting to solve a problem. This helps us focus on the problem at hand while celebrating the good intentions the student has indicated in his or her goals. We can look at how certain behaviors block us from reaching our goals. We can decide on what changes in behavior would help to get back on track.

Preparing to Work Constructively with Parents

Roxanne: If the help and support of parents are needed (as described above), showing parents the student's written goals and contributions to the Respect Agreement (Chapter 4) is a positive way to begin the meeting. I acknowledge how much their child already knows about respect. By starting this way, parents are assured that the teacher knows they have worked with their child to become a respectful person. They do not feel defensive but can heartily join into the process of finding good solutions for their child, for them, and for the teacher. Often such meetings end with smiles and warm handshakes and hope for a better future. I find over and over again that even parents I might have judged as being extremely dysfunctional want good things for their children. The structures that follow in this book help in working with parents—even parents who start out as uncooperative. Parents find that these restorative structures invite them to move along the continuum to being more cooperative. I have found that the process helps them gain new tools and that this inspires them. They often welcome the experience of adding something to their understanding of how to provide their child with structure and discipline.

To illustrate the above, I have had students who not only have a reputation for being difficult but who also have parents with exactly the same reputation. One family with four children spent their time going to three different nearby school districts, and my school was one of those districts. When one or several of the children along with the parents had had so many problems with their current school, they would move. When three of the boys became part of my class three different times, the boys, the parents, and I discovered, because of the structures and practices I had in place, we could work together. Each of the three boys graduated from my eighth-grade class.

This was not without a number of meetings between the boy who was currently in my class, his mother and sometimes his stepfather, and me. One of the boys needed those meetings plus one involving all of the above people and the administration. It was so helpful to have the written goals of the boys at these meetings. Their goals were not the problem. Rather, they lacked strategies for reaching their goals and had practiced strategies for quite a while that actually kept them from learning. This was a challenging situation. The boys were confused. Whenever their mom came to the school in protection mode, it gave them the impression that she somehow approved of their non-cooperative behavior. However, I found the parents and the boys (once they understood what their parents wanted) to be very willing to work with me at making the changes in behavior that led to their being able to remain where they were and to their meeting the academic standards that allowed them to graduate. Caring and a desire for success for her children is really what drove the mother to stand up for them even in ways that were not helpful earlier, but that became helpful as new skills were acquired. I never had the fourth child, a daughter, because the family moved completely out of the area before she got to the eighth grade. I found that I was disappointed not to have the opportunity to continue working with this family.

Concluding Thoughts on Preparation

We teachers need to prepare by clarifying our goals for discipline ahead of time and being ready to articulate and implement those goals with our students and parents. We need to prepare students by giving them the opportunity to articulate their goals as well. Implementing the DTR Flowchart requires preparation.

Chapter 2 • Student/Teacher Conflict

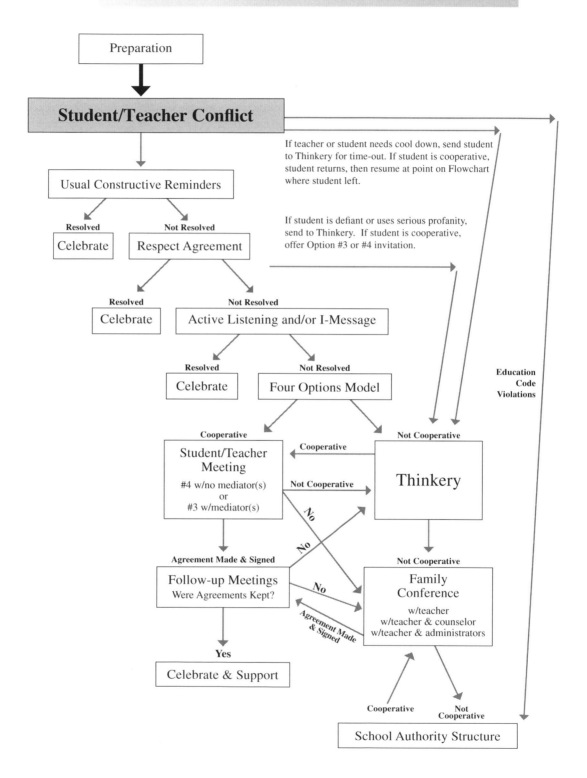

Preparation

Student/Teacher Conflict

If teacher or student needs cool down, send student to Thinkery for time-out. If student is cooperative, student returns, then resume at point on Flowchart where student left.

Usual Constructive Reminders

If student is defiant or uses serious profanity, send to Thinkery. If student is cooperative, offer Option #3 or #4 invitation.

Resolved
Celebrate

Not Resolved
Respect Agreement

Resolved
Celebrate

Not Resolved
Active Listening and/or I-Message

Resolved
Celebrate

Not Resolved
Four Options Model

Education Code Violations

Cooperative
Student/Teacher Meeting
#4 w/no mediator(s)
or
#3 w/mediator(s)

Cooperative

Not Cooperative

Not Cooperative
Thinkery

Not Cooperative

Agreement Made & Signed
Follow-up Meetings
Were Agreements Kept?

No

No

No

Not Cooperative
Family Conference
w/teacher
w/teacher & counselor
w/teacher & administrators

Agreement Made & Signed

Yes
Celebrate & Support

Cooperative

Not Cooperative

School Authority Structure

Copyright © 2008 Ron and Roxanne Claassen

Chapter 2
Student/Teacher Conflict

Introduction

Student/teacher conflict is normal. When it arises, we are at a teachable moment. This is a moment when some real teaching and learning can occur for both the student and the teacher. This is a moment that can become a time of relationship building. What is taught during these times of conflict is what students need as they prepare for their future independent life. Because there will be conflict regardless of which plan for discipline we use, we will use this stop on the Flowchart to gain a better understanding of conflict and conflict theory before we get into what is done at each of the subsequent stops on the Flowchart.

Conflict is a large and stimulating part of our lives. We have found learning about it to be fascinating and helpful. Ron will provide insight into the danger and opportunity of conflict, a definition for conflict, and some basic conflict theory.

Understanding Conflict: The Problem and Some Good News

Ron: Many relationships are damaged, severed, or become ongoing abusive power struggles due to conflicts or injustices that are ignored or managed poorly. Many families, classrooms, and communities experience high stress and low effectiveness due to unresolved conflict. Many parents have students transferred out of classes or schools due to unresolved conflict or violations. Teachers transfer to different schools or leave teaching altogether due to conflict that escalated and was left unresolved. This is true in many workplaces, not just schools. This problem is a pervasive one. It happens at all levels, in our families, workplaces, churches, communities, and nations. It also happens at all times. It is an ancient problem, and it is a current problem. This problem is one that garners intense and broad interest. It has been analyzed and studied extensively, resulting in many ideas, theories, and strategies; yet our schools, in particular, are currently in desperate need of more effective approaches.

The good news is that effective patterns are emerging. Some of these are based on ancient wisdom, and others are from new insights and experiences. This book provides models and strategies that have proven effective in increasing constructive and cooperative responses to conflict while decreasing (but not eliminating) the need for authority and coercion.

The good news is that any teacher who wants to improve effectiveness can learn new patterns for responding rather than simply reacting with the habitual and ineffective patterns. These models and strategies can assist all good teachers in becoming even more effective.

Danger and Opportunity

Ron: When I was first asked, "Which words come to your mind when you think of conflict?" I came up with words like disagreement, anger, frustration, confusion, stress, and hurt feelings, rather than words like trust, agreements, clarity, closeness, and hope. However, as I studied and thought about conflict more, it seemed to me that I wasn't clear about my definition for conflict. I realized that when conflicts were resolved, I dismissed them as not having been conflicts. I only regarded as conflicts those that included harsh words, were painful, and were left unresolved. Because of my definition of conflict and my related feelings, all of which were negative and painful, I naturally wanted to avoid conflict. I began to realize that my way of thinking about conflict was only one option and that there were other ways of viewing conflict.

The Chinese language offers an alternative way of viewing conflict. The symbol for conflict is constructed by putting together two different symbols. When taken together, they may be translated into three different English words: conflict, crisis, or crossroads. The first symbol, on the left, when taken alone is translated into the English word danger. The one on the right is translated into the word opportunity. So, embedded in the language is the suggestion that in every conflict, there is potential for both danger and opportunity. The language construction suggests that every conflict presents crossroads. What the people in the conflict do and what the communities around them in the conflict do will determine whether they experience more danger or opportunity. I find this a challenging idea. It suggests that we as teachers, who experience conflict each day, face a crisis and crossroads in each conflict. Our response to each conflict will influence whether we experience more danger or opportunity.

When reflecting on my past experiences, I remembered a situation that I had not thought of as a conflict, but realized that Roxanne and I, in that conflict situation, had experienced the opportunity rather than the danger. Shortly after being married (1968), we moved to Wusasa, Nigeria, where we set up our first household and lived for three years while I taught mathematics in a secondary school and Roxanne worked in an elementary school. We were assigned to this part of Nigeria due to the shortage of teachers caused by the Nigerian Civil War (referred to in the United States as the Biafra War). In setting up our first household and having just been married, we began discovering some differences that we didn't even know about before our marriage. One difference was that we did not agree about how the toilet paper should be put on the holder. One of us thought that the paper should roll over the top and the other thought it should fall behind and under the roll. I would turn the roll the way I wanted it, and then she would turn it the way she wanted it, etc. This went on for some time without any discussion about it. Reflecting back on that experience, a danger was that we would have argued about it in a way that would create distance between us. Another danger was that one might give in but resent it, again causing a distance between us. An opportunity was that it would become an occasion to communicate, problem solve, and find a good solution. Our journey toward the opportunity started one day when we decided to talk about it (we hadn't studied conflict or been to any conflict resolution training seminars). After some discussion, we agreed to go to a store to look for some toilet paper that was printed with colored patterns or flowers. We hoped that if we found some, we might be able to discern how the manufacturers thought it should be put on the holder, because most likely they would want their design to show to the best advantage. We agreed that if we could determine how the manufacturer thought it should be on the holder, then, for the rest of our married life, we would do it that way. We have now been married for 40 years and are still doing it that way. (If you are curious about which way, the next time you go through the toilet paper aisle, you can do some research.)

Reflecting on this model embedded in the Chinese language, we would both now say that we found the opportunity in that conflict. Because of that conflict and our response to it, our relationship improved a bit, we became closer friends, and we gained confidence that we would be able to discuss the even bigger conflicts that would inevitably emerge, resolve them, and maybe even enjoy the process.

I now believe that all conflicts have the potential to move in either direction. I also believe that while no one person can control the situation entirely, what each person does (those directly involved as well as those who are aware of it and not directly involved) will influence the direction of the relationships affected by the conflict toward either opportunity or danger.

This book is about providing models, strategies, and tools so that a teacher can increase the likelihood of influencing each classroom conflict in ways that maximize the opportunities and minimize the dangers. The danger is that those involved in the conflict emerge from the response to the conflict feeling alienated, damaged, disempowered, less valued, less safe, and acting in ways that are less constructive and cooperative. The opportunity is that the response to the conflict leaves the teacher, students, parents, etc., with increased trust, safety, closeness, and empowerment to act in ways that are more constructive and cooperative in future conflicts that will inevitably emerge.

Defining Conflict

Ron: Conflict is inevitable and normal, but destructive conflict is not. Since we usually name only the painful and unresolved experiences as conflict, it seems odd to say that conflict is normal. When I say that conflict is normal, I am thinking of a particular definition of conflict. Before you read that definition, I would suggest that you might find it helpful to get a few situations in your mind that you would describe as conflicts. When you read the definition, see if the definition fits with your experiences.

Definition: Conflict is not the same thing as disagreement. While most conflicts include disagreement, not all disagreements become conflicts. *A conflict exists when at least one person is blocked or perceives that someone is blocking or attempting to block them from doing or obtaining what they want or that to which think they are entitled.*

Following are some examples of conflicts. Note that each example fits the definition above. I believe that each also presents potential dangers and opportunities. (I am not going to reveal what was done to respond to or resolve the conflicts at this point.)

Example 1: Roxanne and I did not agree about how the toilet paper should be put on the holder. One of us thought that the paper should roll over the top and the other thought it should fall behind and under the roll. This was simply a disagreement and a not a conflict until I began turning the roll the way I wanted it and then she turned it the way she wanted it, and we kept on doing that. Then I was blocking her from having the toilet paper on the roll the way she wanted it, and she was blocking me from having it the way I wanted it. It was the blocking that made the disagreement into a conflict.

Example 2: I was teaching a class of teachers about conflict resolution. Two of them always came in late in the morning and stayed out longer from breaks. I was being blocked from starting on time with everyone present. If I waited until they came in, I was blocking the others who were there on time from using those precious minutes for learning. I suspect that the ones coming in late thought I was blocking them from what it was they wanted to do that caused them to come in late. The dangers were that in whatever way I responded, I might damage my relationship with those who were late or with those ready to start. The opportunity was that it would become an occasion for learning together and be done in a way that would build all our relationships.

Example 3: Roxanne and I were on vacation at Bass Lake. It had been a warm day that began to cool off in the early evening. She stated that she was going to open the door to let some of that wonderful cool air in. I responded that I wanted the door closed. This became a conflict when my preference blocked or attempted to block her from opening the door. A conflict like this is normal. The question was, how would we respond? Would we find the danger or the opportunity? A danger was that we would argue about it or one might give in but resent it. A danger was that we might respond to each other in ways that would ruin our vacation or even damage our relationship. The opportunity was that this conflict would become an occasion to communicate, to problem solve, and to find a good solution. The opportunity was that we would respond in ways that would improve our relationship and we would become closer.

Example 4: A twelve-year-old boy climbed up on his roof with a BB gun and shot at two of the windows in his neighbor's house. The neighbor found out that the twelve-year-old did it. This was a conflict. It was also a violation and an injustice.

A danger was that nothing would be done and the boy would not accept responsibility and perhaps get a wrong impression about right and wrong behavior. Another danger was that the neighbor would be filled with anger and resentment toward the boy and his parents, which would cause ongoing tension in their relationship as neighbors. A danger was that the reasons for the boy doing what he did would never be addressed. A danger was that the boy would be severely punished, perhaps beyond what he thought appropriate, and in response, he would decide that he was going to get even with those who punished him. A danger was that the response would cause the neighbors' relationship to deteriorate and they would actively find ways to "get even." An opportunity was that because of what happened, the boy would accept responsibility and make things right between them. An opportunity was that the reasons for the behavior would be discussed and addressed. An opportunity was that because of the response to the conflict, the relationship between the neighbors would improve.

Example 5: It was time for class to start. A student took a cap from under his shirt and put it in his desk. The school rule said that students were not to bring caps to school. The teacher confronted the student and asked for the cap. The student had been given permission by the security person to put the cap under his shirt and then in his desk. The student refused to give the cap to the teacher. This was a conflict, according to our definition. The student's act of bringing the cap was a violation of the school rule, and the teacher's request was blocking the student from keeping the cap in his desk. The question at that point was how would the teacher and student respond? A danger was a heated and destructive argument between the teacher and student. A danger was a report to security (not the one who gave the boy permission) and forced removal of the boy from the classroom. A danger was angry resistance from the boy to the removal. A danger was that because of what happened, the relationship between the teacher and student would be damaged and because of that, each would experience increased stress and less cooperation with each other in school. A danger was that many future learning opportunities would be missed. An opportunity was that they would listen to each other and problem-solve a mutually agreeable solution. An opportunity was that because of what happened they would each gain respect for each other. An opportunity was that because of the response to the conflict, they would be more cooperative with each other in the future, experience less stress, and be more open to learning from each other.

The purpose of these examples is to illustrate the definition of conflict. Conflict is not just disagreement but must include blocking. Many disagreements don't include blocking and therefore do not become conflict. In *every* conflict there is potential danger and opportunity, for each party and for their relationship. Conflict is inevitable and normal. Many conflicts are mutual, while some are clearly violations or injustices. Often even conflicts that are mutual feel to each side like the other is the offender. The responses to the conflict are what will determine whether they move more in the danger or opportunity direction. In every conflict in a classroom, the teacher's response influences if the student and the class experience more danger or opportunity.

The purpose of this book is to equip teachers to identify conflict, reduce the dangers, and increase the opportunities in every conflict within the classroom or school. Before we look at the management models and resolution strategies, it is critical that leaders recognize the value of consciously addressing conflict in the early stages rather than allowing them to escalate.

Unmanaged Conflict: Escalation

Ron: Conflict that is not effectively managed follows a very predictable escalation pattern. As it escalates, the dangers emerge and the opportunities seem more remote. Conflict that is properly managed does not follow this *unmanaged escalation cycle*. The reason for introducing this model is to encourage you as a teacher to be more conscious of how conflict escalates if the conflict is not consciously and deliberately managed.

As you read the stages and follow the diagram, allow your mind to wander as the comments cause you to remember your own experiences. Have you ever experienced anything that resembles this?

Stage I

Conflict (blocking) usually starts in a situation of change. Students are transitioning from assignment to assignment, to lunch, to another class, etc. A new student joins the classroom. The teacher is absent, and a substitute is with the class. The list could go on and on.

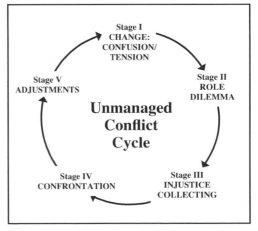

If, as part of the change dynamic, someone experiences blocking, there is then a conflict. It would be wonderful at this point if our conflict management habits would cause us to work on it and clarify and resolve the confusion so that the tension, a natural response to blocking, could be reduced. But that is not the way it works in an unmanaged conflict cycle.

Since it is an unmanaged conflict cycle, the early indicators of a developing conflict are ignored. Often one unconsciously tries just to get the indicators to go away. We might take a pill for the tension or rationalize away the confusion. Some have sayings to help them avoid the conflict such as, "Let's not make a mountain out of a molehill," or "It's probably no big deal."

Because the conflict (the blocking or perception of blocking) is not consciously recognized and dealt with, the tension and confusion increase and cause the parties to move on to the next stage in the cycle.

Stage II

As the tension and confusion increase, the questions escalate. "What am I doing to cause this tension?" "What is he or she doing to cause this tension?" "Why did he or she do that?" "Who is in charge here, anyway?" And finally, "Who's at fault here?"

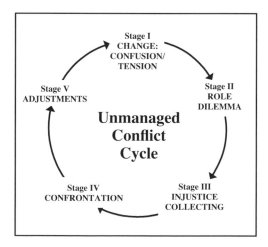

When one gets to this question regarding fault, the tendency is to answer it quite quickly. It's obvious—it's always the other person. Once fault has been determined, last week's actions suddenly make more sense. "Now I understand why he or she did that!" Once fault has been determined, one watches him or her through the "fault lens," which filters out the good and focuses on the things he or she does that are wrong.

By answering the "fault" question early, one is subconsciously attempting to get out of confusion. "The problem is now obvious! I'm no longer confused! The problem is not me, it is you!"

Stage III

Now that fault has been determined, one pays attention to the wrongs and injustices and remembers them. "Ouch, you shouldn't have said that. I'm not going to say anything about it now, but I will remember it!" Convinced that things can only get worse, one now collects the "ammunition" that will be needed later. It is time to prepare for the confrontation. This stage generates a great deal of negative energy.

The original change that started this cycle has probably been forgotten by now. Even if it could be remembered, it would seem irrelevant at this point because the focus is now on the injustices and especially the most recent injustice. Because it is not a conscious and managed process, a *confrontation* is likely to emerge.

Stage IV

This stage is an unplanned and unmanaged confrontation. I emphasize the "unplanned" because it usually happens at a time that is very inconvenient for at least one of the parties. For example it may happen when a teacher is trying to start a lesson, a teacher is just about to leave home for work, a staff meeting has just about ended and the others want to go home, or the meeting has ended and it happens out in the parking lot. It is "unmanaged" because what happens here is that one of the injustices, maybe a small one, just sneaks out. The other person may respond with a defensive statement but more likely with one of the injustices he or she has been collecting. The next ones are a little bigger and the pattern continues. As it continues it gets louder. Speaking loudly, sometimes yelling, is an unconscious response when one thinks the other is not listening. Speaking loudly is an unconscious attempt to get the other to listen.

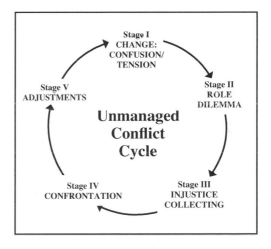

This discharge of parallel monologues gets louder and more intense. But it doesn't come to a resolution. It just runs out of steam and ends. In some ways it feels better since the collected injustices are now out in the open. And in some ways it feels worse for the same reason. With the collected injustices out in the open and with the lack of resolution, it is time for an adjustment.

Stage V

The most common adjustment in conflict is distance. Perhaps distance is used so much because there is an immediate payoff—it reduces the tension. At first the distance may just take the form of not talking or perhaps avoiding each other. Those who live together may spend less time together or find things to do away from home. At home, distance may take the form of watching television more to avoid talking so much. Those who work together may just schedule things so that breaks are at different times,

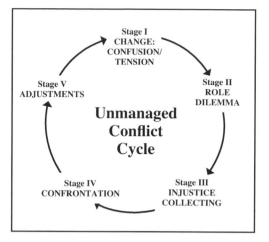

or one might ask to be transferred or have the other one transferred. A student at first may try to avoid the teacher and the teacher might avoid the student. Later the student or teacher may request that the student be transferred to a different class.

Distance is a common way of responding to conflict but it doesn't heal the wounds, it doesn't repair the damages, and it doesn't address the problem that initially brought on the confusion. If, in spite of the distance, the conflicted parties are still in the same classroom, living in the same house, or working at the same job, it won't be long until there is a new change, accompanying tension and confusion, and the cycle starts over.

Round Two, Three, Four, etc.

Each cycle speeds up. The new "blocking" and accompanying tension and confusion (Stage I) stimulate the memory of "I know who is at fault" (Stage II). Each simply remembers the old injustices and adds new injustices (Stage III). There may be another confrontation (Stage IV) or it might be skipped over and distance added (Stage V). If there is a confrontation (Stage IV) it is very likely that it will sound almost exactly like the first since each feels like the other was not listening the first time. Once one gets spinning on this "unmanaged conflict cycle," it is very hard to get off.

At the beginning of this section, I asked you to consider, "Have you ever experienced anything like this?" If your experiences are similar to mine and to those in my seminars, your immediate response is most likely an emphatic, "Have I ever!!!" I know how you feel. The first time I saw this model (actually a slightly different cycle by Norman Shawchuck), I wondered if he had been following me around. I was very surprised. I had always thought all my conflicts were unique. I was amazed to see many of my conflicts had followed such a predictable pattern.

There is a high cost for families, schools, businesses, and organizations where conflict is not consciously managed. This unmanaged cycle is common. Distance is a very costly way of dealing with conflicts, both emotionally and financially. In schools, it also impedes academic progress.

When a teacher and student are spinning on the cycle, a great deal of energy that could be used for productive work is diverted to thinking about the next confrontation or about how to avoid it. Because of their unresolved conflict, when the student needs help to work efficiently and effectively, he or she avoids the direct consultation and gives up or wastes time trying to find the information in other ways. If one asks for a transfer, the costs include time for administrators to listen and make a decision whether a transfer should be granted. If a transfer is granted, there is lost time and substantial energy in the need for establishing new relationships.

Students and teachers who spin on this cycle experience deep pain. Their expectations are that their relationship should be very different. Distance reduces the open tension but it makes it worse in other ways. The unmanaged conflict cycles or resulting separations are very costly emotionally and financially for the two involved. They are also very costly for the class, due to lost learning time and increased stress.

These examples illustrate just a few of the costs of not recognizing an escalating conflict. The costs are high for a teacher who doesn't recognize an escalating conflict. The good news is that teachers who understand the costs of unmanaged conflict can learn to recognize the early stages of conflict and take constructive action to minimize the dangers and maximize the opportunities.

Roxanne's Experience

Roxanne: Building community heads me down the left side of the Flowchart. This is the side of the chart that leads to constructive action and to maximizing the opportunities provided by conflict. It is good to begin the year with this structure. It is also possible to institute the structure at any point in the year that you learn of it and want to use it. I tell my students in detail what I am doing. I show them the Flowchart and the models, and I teach them the strategies I plan to use. I might also tell them that Ron and I were developing a restorative structure to solve conflicts in schools, and I wanted to try the ideas with them and hear what they thought about them. Ron's seminar attendees often tell the students in their classrooms that they have a homework assignment and need their students' help to complete it. However one approaches putting the structure into place, my experience is that kids are very interested in how we are going to work at our conflicts and enjoy being part of figuring it out (problem solving is part of the required standards in reading, math, science, etc.).

A classroom is a group, and as Dr. Bruce Tuckman says, groups go through stages. At the beginning of the year, the class is forming. There is a period of time that the students look to me, as the leader of the group, to guide them in the process of formation. Students are figuring out what their place is in this new group, and they need and want my leadership. I, as the teacher, am the leader who establishes the norm that says all of them are very important and valuable as members of the group. We are also deciding on what the norms will be that will guide our community life together. The Respect Agreement stop on the Flowchart (Chapter 4) is a process for establishing our norms.

Once the structure and procedures are established, the group does not need as much of my direct leadership. I experience students taking on some of the leadership themselves. As they gain confidence in the structure and procedures, many of them are able to do much of it on their own—they monitor themselves and others and approach problems themselves using the established procedures. Toward the end of the year, the group realizes that we are approaching an ending time. I find the class once again needing some strong leadership from me as they enter this stage.

There are more student/teacher meetings at the beginning of the year as we are getting established as a class. A few students need to go all the way down to the Family Conference (Chapter 10) on the Flowchart to experience discipline that restores and to decide if they are going to be cooperative. These meetings lead to greater cooperation by students who often come to class with a reputation for having behavioral problems. There are fewer student/teacher meetings as the structure is established and understood by the class. On occasions when there is going to be a fairly long break, such as the winter holiday, there seems to be a need for a few more meetings than usual, as some students experience these times as stressful and confusing for reasons that are many and varied. The end of the year (the last three or four weeks) seems to be another time that the most difficult students need to find out whether all the norms established are still in place.

It has been far easier to get through these natural times of transition and to experience the opportunities of conflict with the structure of the Flowchart in place. There used to be one or two eighth-grade students each year who pushed the old punishment structure to the point where they were not allowed to participate in the activities leading up to graduation or the graduation itself. This was not only punishment for the student, but parents experienced it as punishment as well. With the DTR structure in place, we have not needed to exclude anyone from the end-of-the-year activities or graduation. We have had some agreements with students that have been very creative and that students have fulfilled in order to take responsibility as well as be accountable for their actions. These have allowed them to move on from our school feeling restored, respected, and reintegrated. A good understanding of conflict has enabled me to see conflict as an opportunity for growth and understanding and to pass this vision along to my students.

Chapter 3 • **Usual Constructive Reminders**

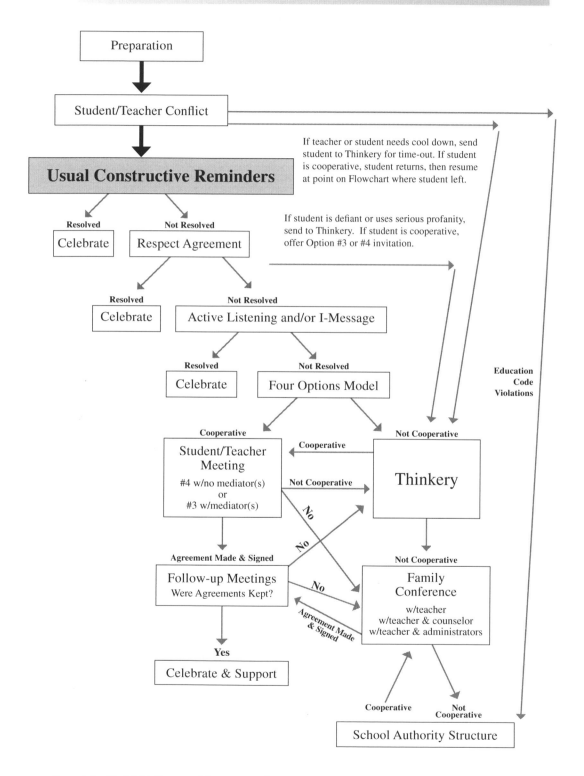

Preparation

Student/Teacher Conflict

If teacher or student needs cool down, send student to Thinkery for time-out. If student is cooperative, student returns, then resume at point on Flowchart where student left.

Usual Constructive Reminders

Resolved — Celebrate

Not Resolved — Respect Agreement

If student is defiant or uses serious profanity, send to Thinkery. If student is cooperative, offer Option #3 or #4 invitation.

Resolved — Celebrate

Not Resolved — Active Listening and/or I-Message

Resolved — Celebrate

Not Resolved — Four Options Model

Education Code Violations

Cooperative — Student/Teacher Meeting
#4 w/no mediator(s)
or
#3 w/mediator(s)

Cooperative

Not Cooperative — Thinkery

Not Cooperative

Agreement Made & Signed — Follow-up Meetings
Were Agreements Kept?

No

No

No

Agreement Made & Signed

Not Cooperative — Family Conference
w/teacher
w/teacher & counselor
w/teacher & administrators

Yes — Celebrate & Support

Cooperative

Not Cooperative

School Authority Structure

Copyright © 2008 Ron and Roxanne Claassen

Chapter 3
Usual Constructive Reminders

"Usual Constructive Reminders" are used more often than any other stop on the DTR Flowchart. What exactly are usual constructive reminders? As we continue down the Flowchart with strategies on how student/teacher conflict can be worked at in a restorative way, this point is where we spend most of our time with most students because most of our students do come to us ready to learn. Usual constructive reminders are the small, almost imperceptible things we do to get someone who is going off track back on track. With practice and experience, we become very good at successfully carrying out these reminders. When they are skillfully employed, they ensure that students do not get the wrong idea about what is appropriate because the reminders happen as soon as the misbehavior is starting. These usual constructive reminders will be carried out respectfully only if we as teachers have prepared ourselves to be constructive, even if a student doesn't reciprocate.

Roxanne: My usual constructive reminders include things such as looking in the direction of a disturbance and very slightly shaking my head to indicate that I want whatever is happening to stop. It helps for this to be done with a pleasant look on my face rather than an angry look. Another thing I do is to walk over near the student who needs my attention and simply stand there while continuing to teach the lesson until the student stops and gets back on track. When necessary, I make eye contact (not the "evil eye") to let the student know I am aware of the off-task activity and that I don't want he or she to miss what we are doing as a class.

Another type of usual constructive reminder is directly saying to the entire class, "You will want to write this down in your notes," and then continuing the lesson while looking around the room to see if that got the students who were off task back on task. I can vary that direct statement with whatever behavior I am encouraging students to practice. For example: "You will really want to listen carefully to this." "Here is a process you will need to know later so copy it down exactly as I put it on the board." "Be sure you are looking at page such and such because that is where we are reading right now." "Read along in your book, it will help you get the information," etc.

Usual constructive reminders include being super aware and monitoring things such as whether someone needs a pencil or an eraser and having those items handy for students to borrow when needed. I find having a container full of nice sharpened pencils with good erasers is very constructive and shows how much I care. They often show respect back to me by bringing their own pencils the next day and returning the borrowed ones because they know I appreciate having the pencils available for as long as possible. Keeping paper at hand and taking a sheet to a student I want to be taking notes is another way of reminding. If I am doing this respectfully and out of care and concern because I want the student to do well, students experience these reminders that way and not as a negative "I am mad at you."

It is very important to develop this skill because you do not want to be permissive about behavior that will keep students from learning. I find quite often that students are discussing what I am teaching when they begin talking to one another. In these cases, I directly say to the whole class, "Please don't talk yet. I will give you a chance to discuss this in a moment. If you could just hold your comments to each other for a bit longer, you will have a chance to ask questions and share ideas." In my usual constructive reminders, I have found it best to assume that my students are seeking to do what they are supposed to do because that is most often the case. There is a common belief that we get what we expect from students, so expecting positive, constructive behavior is likely to elicit that kind of behavior.

Walking around the room and letting all the students know you are aware of them and what they are doing is also a usual constructive reminder. It has been amusing and helpful to realize that there are some students who genuinely do not think I am talking to them when I am addressing the entire class. I make sure to stand close to them and make eye contact with them a little more. As I walk around and present material, many students put away notes they were planning to pass to another and take out their real notes again. This invites them to self-monitor. I do not need to say a thing to a student who self-monitors in this way. In fact, I can give them a slight nod or smile of approval as I walk near them. This "celebration" is on the Flowchart. Students let me know they appreciate this by returning an appreciative look that says they recognize they are back on track.

Another type of usual constructive reminder can be what you put on the walls in your classroom. At the beginning of the year, I put up on the walls all the writing about goals that my students have done with a collage about themselves. Nodding in the direction of those also invites students to remember and begin doing what needs to be done.

Usual constructive reminders also work in situations when you want to give students time to work on new material in class. Some students have a difficult time setting about a new task. When students are working on their own or in small groups, usual constructive reminders can be a bit more direct because you can talk directly to students about remembering agreements and goals. I like to have as many of these factors as possible (goals, models, strategies, respect agreement) visually available to students so we can point and make decisions with or without speaking. Some students need to learn that the reason you are having them work in class is so they can become more familiar with that which is new and so they can ask questions and gain as much understanding as possible before going off on their own to do the homework. Usual constructive reminders are also times of informing students about the "why" behind the requirements.

I find this kind of contact with students to be energizing and stimulating. They experience it this way as well. I know this because the atmosphere remains relaxed, and students are happy and comfortable. If the usual constructive reminders do not solve the conflict, the Flowchart continues us on the journey to find ways to reach students and build relationships so we can enable them to reach their goals. The Flowchart leads us in a constructive escalation so problems get solved and relationships remain good.

Chapter 4 is about the respect agreement. Once that is made and posted, it becomes another usual constructive reminder. If I am losing the attention of a lot of students, I include it in the reminders by walking over to the agreement and briefly inviting them to remember their agreements before going on with a lesson. It is a visual that all of us have signed indicating our intention to be respectful of each other. The next chapter describes this respect agreement stop on the Flowchart in detail.

Chapter 4 • **Respect Agreement**

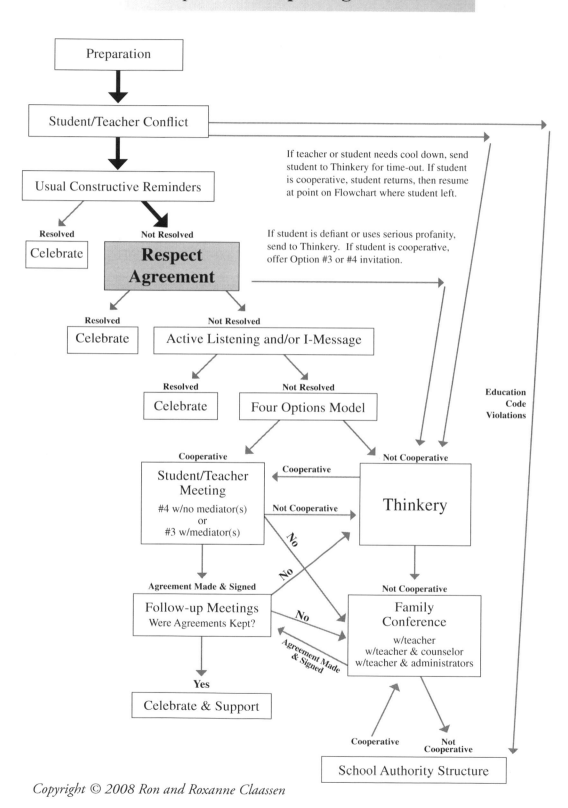

Preparation

Student/Teacher Conflict

Usual Constructive Reminders

If teacher or student needs cool down, send student to Thinkery for time-out. If student is cooperative, student returns, then resume at point on Flowchart where student left.

Resolved

Celebrate

Not Resolved

Respect Agreement

If student is defiant or uses serious profanity, send to Thinkery. If student is cooperative, offer Option #3 or #4 invitation.

Resolved

Celebrate

Not Resolved

Active Listening and/or I-Message

Resolved

Celebrate

Not Resolved

Four Options Model

Education Code Violations

Cooperative

Student/Teacher Meeting

#4 w/no mediator(s)
or
#3 w/mediator(s)

Cooperative

Not Cooperative

Thinkery

Not Cooperative

Not Cooperative

No

No

Agreement Made & Signed

Follow-up Meetings

Were Agreements Kept?

No

Not Cooperative

Family Conference

w/teacher
w/teacher & counselor
w/teacher & administrators

Agreement Made & Signed

Yes

Celebrate & Support

Cooperative

Not Cooperative

School Authority Structure

Copyright © 2008 Ron and Roxanne Claassen

Chapter 4
Respect Agreement

Introduction

As we move along the DTR Flowchart, we come to another important stop on this guide to creating a constructive, cooperative classroom community. Even though it is not in the center of the chart, we have found the Respect Agreement central to beginning to institute restorative practices. Roxanne began using this lesson nine years ago and says it is difficult to imagine, from her perspective now, not using it to get a group of learners and her off to a good start. It is effective with primary, intermediate, middle school, and high school classrooms. The Respect Agreement is also being used between teachers, classified staff, and administration. At Fresno Pacific University it is being used in dorm living units with resident assistants and students. We also have reports of families creating their own respect agreement and renewing it annually.

Roxanne: My school, which is K–8, has intentionally used this lesson in each classroom to get the year off to a good start. It works! Once the agreement is established, it is like a whistle on the playground (only better). You know how you can blow your whistle out on a playground with 200–300 students present? The ones who are tackling, wrestling, throwing the ball at each other rather than to each other, kissing under the tree, posturing as if about to fight, hitting each other with their coat sleeves, etc., will all stop and look at you. The Respect Agreement becomes like that in the classroom, except it is a quiet and compelling reminder for all of us to be responsible and accountable. By just walking near the Respect Agreement hanging on the wall I send a message to the ones who are disturbing others and themselves. They know instinctively that I am indirectly addressing them. I even get the attention of some I had not realized were drifting. The beauty of it is, often I do not even need to say anything. It talks to them for me because it invites them to talk to themselves and reminds them of what they need to be doing.

Developing a respect agreement gets an entire class writing and thinking about respect. This means everyone, including the ones who have a reputation for not being respectful. The first time I used this lesson and put up the composite of everyone's ideas (I used to take their quick-writes and make the composite myself—I have since changed this), I was accused by the student with the worst reputation of making up the ideas myself and just putting up the ones that I particularly liked. Luckily I had their quick-writes in my hand. I asked the class if it would be all right for me to read a few of them directly without mentioning the names of the writers. Then I asked my confronter if he would mind if I found his and read it. With a knowing smile on his face, he decided he did not want me to do that. I read a few more without saying who had written them. It occurred to me that it might be important to recognize with the class that they all knew a lot about respect and that that was a good thing. I did this. My confronter and I developed a very stimulating relationship. He enjoyed being kept on his toes and keeping me on my toes. I let him know I was ready to keep up with him with a spirit of enjoyment of the challenge.

I believe that in my decision to be unconditionally constructive (first stop on the Flowchart, Preparation), I am deciding to respect myself, my students, and others (and this ends up affecting all one's relationships). Because respect is so central, this is a wonderful place for a new class to begin. However, I have also found this does not have to be done only at the beginning of a new school year. It is effective whenever you decide you want to do it.

Respect Agreement Lesson Plan

Following the Respect Agreement lesson plan, you and the class can develop your own agreement about how you are going to show each other respect. This agreement is a first step in beginning the process of building trust, for, as Ron says, "It is in making and keeping agreements that trust is built." Respect and trust enable a learning community to take the chances that need to be taken for maximum learning to occur. We often learn the most from our mistakes. If we can make our mistakes in an atmosphere of respect, we are much more likely to learn positive things from them.

The lesson plan is incredibly simple, yet I know what it asks us to consider and do is not that simple. Experience has taught me that some students come to class knowing how to act and what to do to be respectful, and they do these things. Others come to class knowing what to do but not having decided to do what is required to be respectful. I have found that both groups become active and willing participants in this lesson. Just as some come with high academic goals and few constructive strategies to meet them, some also come without well-developed social strategies for being respectful. This is a teachable moment for all of us.

Developing a Respect Agreement with each new class has made a huge difference in me, my students, our attitudes, and the way we treat each other. It gives us a concrete way to begin building community. Here is what I do: At the beginning of each year, we look at the concept of respect and determine what respect will look like in our classroom. First, we brainstorm individually. I invite them to fold their paper into four sections and label these sections: students respecting themselves and other students, students respecting staff, teacher/staff respecting students, all respecting the equipment (building, tables, chairs, books, etc,) and facilities. I tell them to write what they think respect would look/sound like in these four areas. (I don't give examples or

Student Respecting Student	Student Respecting Teacher
Teacher Respecting Student	All Respecting Equipment & Facilities

more instruction because I want them to struggle with and write down their own ideas.) Often this generates lots of thought and questions about respect as students try to figure out what to write. You may have students who are at first surprised that you are inviting them to say what they think a teacher should do to respect students. (The first few times I did this, they were surprised because they had never before been asked to say what a teacher respecting a student might look like. Now that we do it in all classes, they come expecting and appreciating this opportunity.) They are grateful for this chance because they know that to get respect, people (teachers or other adults) need to give respect. I welcome any questions or comments about respect and keep putting them back to my students, encouraging them to start writing their ideas.

Once we are all finished writing (I write, too), we meet in table groups (four to five in each group) to share the ideas we have written. My first instruction for each table group is to invite each student in the group to read what they have written. Next, I pass out a large piece of chart paper to each group. One group member writes all the ideas represented by their group on the chart paper. There is a delightful buzz in the room as the groups seriously think and talk about respect. My ideas are

Just keep all ideas? More precise — more help...

also included because I join one of the groups. In nine years, I have not found any students wanting to sit silently—they all get involved. Next each group decides on a spokesperson who will share their list. The group lists are hung where everyone can see all of the lists.

At this point I am somewhat awestruck at how much they all already know about respect. I take advantage of this to compliment them. I let them know that I think they are wonderful, and they have had wonderful parents, grandparents, aunts, uncles, and/or teachers who have all done an excellent job in teaching them about respect. It truly is impressive to see what results from this exercise. We talk about the idea that knowing all this is different from deciding to do what we know and having the strategies to carry out what we know. I tell them I want us to consider all of these ideas and choose the ones we want to include in our respect agreement that we will make with each other to clarify how we will be a respectful community.

We make these choices in a variety of ways. One that works well is to have each group mark four of their ideas that they think are the most important to have as part of our agreement. Then we start making our class list by writing four ideas from the first group. The next group checks to see if any of those are the same as the ones they have chosen. If not, we add four from that group. If they are the same, or one of them is the same, they choose another from their list that is important to them. This goes on until all have had the chance to add all ideas from each group to our composite list. I usually have about seven or eight groups. Next, we ask ourselves if there is anything anyone feels strongly about that needs to be added that is not yet part of our list. I ask them if it is okay for me to take the ideas we have generated and write them into a form that can be the basis of our respect agreement.

I take all of their chart papers and make the composite list. Earlier agreements were written such that I assumed I was making the agreement along with them. Now, I follow a form that explicitly divides the list into what I, the teacher, am agreeing to do, what they, the students, are agreeing to do in terms of themselves and each other and the teachers/staff, and what all of us agree to do in terms of the facilities and the equipment. I write the ideas on chart paper, large enough so everyone can see it, with the title, "Our Respect Agreement" or "We can create a respectful, cooperative classroom and school by:" (some agreement examples appear later). Then we look at the list and decide together whether all would be willing to sign our respect agreement.

Every year there is at least one student who wants to know what will happen if he or she does not sign the agreement. I welcome this as an indication that they do not lightly sign their names to things without being sure they can keep their word. They understand that this is something we are going to do; these are not just ideas that will hang on the wall. Their question indicates that they understand this. That is where I start with students who have this concern. I open this up to others who might want to join the discussion.

Our agreement usually includes not chewing gum because that is a school rule. One year this was the item that caused several to pause before they signed. We discussed in detail why this is an item of respect (the custodian is the person left to clean up gum that does not get into the trash can; there are examples of spots on the rug and sidewalk that do not look good at all). We also talked about this being our ideal while realizing we are not all perfect. I had the opportunity to assure them once again of my commitment to be constructive with each conflict situation that might arise. I recognized this as an example of that possibility and got to describe what I envisioned happening (by showing them the Flowchart) if one of them did not keep the agreement. We imagined together all of the reminders and finally us sitting down, talking, and working on the problem together if it continued to be a problem. Our goal would be to find a solution that was good for all of us (perhaps even including the custodian).

None of this is wasted time. I know we are all concerned about teaching all of the state standards and improving test scores. Processing a violation of the respect agreement addresses several state standards. Last year, when each class had created their own respect agreement, our test scores significantly improved. Although I do not have quantitative evidence, I believe the test scores are better because of DTR. Processing the gum-chewing issue with that student and the rest of the class was a teaching/learning opportunity that saved a lot of time later (actually providing additional teaching time and greater academic cooperation). That student signed the agreement, did not chew gum, and ended the year meeting his academic goals.

Our agreements have caused us to look seriously at the school rules. Students, parents, teachers, and administrators have talked about some of the rules and have been willing to adjust rules that are impossible to enforce evenly and fairly throughout the school. Currently we are working on the gum rule and trying to figure out how to adjust it so students can chew gum responsibly, since it is clear the rule is not being followed the same way in each classroom. Some teachers are strict, and others lenient to the point of occasionally offering gum as a treat. On the other hand, it's important that the custodial staff not have to spend increased time cleaning gum off of carpet and sidewalks. I think we will come up with some creative ways to resolve this. I have included this unresolved situation because it illustrates that our staff has realized that there is value and stimulation in re-examining rules when there is an interest, staff or students, in addressing a situation in more creative ways.

A student wondering whether to sign also gives me the opportunity to talk with them about my own struggles with doing what I know to be right as my first response rather than my second or third response. We discuss how we can all help one another by continuing to invite respect (be willing to throw the gum away if you are caught with it) if someone is not keeping the agreement. We discuss how we can view these times as learning opportunities.

Examples of Respect Agreements

Following are some examples of actual respect agreements. The first example is of an earlier agreement when I did not specify categories. The second example explicitly divides the list into what I, the teacher, am agreeing to do, what they, the students, are agreeing to do in terms of themselves and each other, and in terms of the teachers/staff, and what all of us agree to do in terms of the facilities and the equipment.

Here is an example of an early respect agreement:

We can create a respectful, cooperative class and school by:

1. Treating others the way you want to be treated.
2. Listening.
3. Having and using good manners.
4. Acting with maturity.
5. Being prepared (books, homework, pencils, and open mind).
6. Being responsible for the equipment and the facilities.
7. Complimenting each other.
8. Raising your hand before speaking.
9. Not talking out of turn.
10. Not talking back.
11. Not talking when the teacher is talking.

12.   Not making fun of people.

13.   Being positive (having a positive attitude).

14.   Asking before we borrow and returning what we borrow.

15.   Respecting diversity (race, culture, traditions, beliefs).

16.   Not using profanity.

17.   Being open to learning new things.

I am willing to be respectful and cooperative:

(Each student and the teacher sign the agreement when they are satisfied that doing these things will create a respectful learning environment.)

Here is a more recent example of a respect agreement in which we clearly defined each of the four categories:

We can create a respectful/cooperative classroom and school by:

The Teacher Respecting Students

- Talk in a calm voice.
- Be careful not to embarrass students.
- Help when someone needs help.
- Problem solve—don't give dirty looks.
- Guide discussions—decide with students how all will participate and be heard (small groups, raise hands, draw names, etc.).
- Be careful when using a whistle.
- Be polite.
- Be prepared.
- Pay attention to students and their ideas.

The Students Respecting the Teacher

- Listen without talking; pay attention.
- Don't talk during a test.
- Be careful not to embarrass the teacher.
- Listen with an open mind.
- Be prepared and ready to learn.
- Problem solve—don't give dirty looks.
- Be polite and nice.
- Ask if you need to borrow something and return it.

The Students Respecting Themselves and Other Students
- Don't talk during a test.
- Do your own work.
- Ask before you borrow something and return it.
- Treat each other the way you want to be treated (with respect).
- Avoid profanity, gum, or seeds.
- Listen to each other; pay attention.
- Keep your hands to yourself.
- Problem solve—don't give dirty looks.
- Stay quiet for each other.
- Pick up after yourself.
- Show new students around the school.
- Be polite and nice.
- Respect the property of others.

All of Us Respecting the School Facilities and Equipment
- Put trash in the trash cans.
- No chewing gum or eating seeds.
- Don't run in the classroom.
- Take good care of the books (keep them covered, don't write in them).
- Don't write on the furniture or the walls.
- Repair, replace, or clean what you ruin.

I am willing to be respectful and cooperative:

(Each student and the teacher sign the agreement when they are satisfied that doing these things will create a respectful learning environment.)

Each step of the creating process of a respect agreement causes us to read and think about respect multiple times and in multiple ways. It is helpful to think about these things out in the open and intentionally. As we work on deciding what will be in the final respect agreement, I make sure the original small group charts stay up to continue to remind us that these are ideas we have discerned together. As a step to completing the agreement, I let my students know that I am willing to do what is on the list as the teacher/leader of this learning community and that I am willing to sign the agreement. I ask each of them to consider if they are willing to sign, meaning that they would be committing themselves to doing their best to keep the agreement.

I put the final form of the agreement on a large sheet and put it in a place with markers and invite them to sign. Again if there is someone who is not ready to sign, we either ponder the student's concerns together as group or I work with the student individually. (I encourage including parents if the kids would like that—they rarely do.) With a student who is reluctant to sign, we think about what the class would be like if we were all willing to do the things on the list and what it would be like if we did not do the things on the list. This kind of challenge seems to serve to strengthen the idea of the respect agreement as a good and important goal to have for ourselves as a classroom community and encourages the reluctant ones to sign willingly. My experience is that most sign immediately and even the reluctant ones sign soon, after a little more consideration. Once the agreement is signed, it is posted in a prominent spot in the room, and left up for the entire school year.

I have been doing this for nine years. It has made such a positive difference in how our relationships develop throughout the school year. I teach eighth graders, who can be very challenging when they want to be. There has not been a class to this point where there was someone unwilling, after the process is completed, to sign the agreement. The agreements become such an important part of our lives together that I find myself wanting to save them as reminders of each group much like parents save baby shoes to remind them of where their child began and the growth they experienced together.

How the Respect Agreement Is Used

Now that the agreement is made and posted, I guide the way it becomes central to our life together. In the first two weeks of school, I start each day by reading or inviting a student to read the agreement as a reminder to all of us of our intention to be respectful and cooperative. If they wonder why we are doing this each day, I tell them the process of developing the agreement is helpful in establishing a climate of respect, but it is not magical. All of us have habits we have formed. Some of our habits are good and help us be students who can make academic and social progress. Some of our habits are not helpful and can prevent us from reaching our goals. Some habits of responding are difficult to overcome. The respect agreement names the things we want to do to show respect.

The class and I figure out together what some of those habits might be that annoy others, or keep them and ourselves from learning, such as tapping a pencil or foot, drawing on someone else's binder or paper, humming or whistling at inappropriate times, talking constantly when others want to listen to the teacher or other students, giving disrespectful looks, needing frequently to use someone else's pencils or pens, not being prepared, etc. We discuss how we can use the agreement to remind ourselves of what we would like to do in our relationships with each other. I let them know that after the first two weeks I will not continue reading the agreement each day, but I will refer to it when needed and will invite them to refer to it when some of us are not keeping it. I tell them this will be less often if we all get a good feel for what we have agreed by reading the agreement together for a couple of weeks. This does not take up a lot of time, but is a valuable part of establishing the norms as our community is forming.

The agreement makes it so I do not have to tell a student I don't like what they are doing. I ask them to consider whether or not what they are doing is part of our agreement. I ask if they are planning to keep our agreement. It is not just me expecting something. They are invited to expect something, too. This can include expecting things of me as well. I usually have to ask directly if they think there is some part of the agreement I am not keeping. They are often too polite or just unused to calling an adult to accountability to do this right away on their own.

Respect Agreement Stories

A couple of examples will give a feel for how I do this.

Patricia was sending messages to her friend across the room with her eyes and gestures that were disturbing and distracting to me and a number of students between her and her friend. I was introducing new material, and I wanted everyone to have the chance to get it. I stopped and walked over to the Respect Agreement on the wall. I said something like, "Before we go any further with this lesson, maybe we should read our agreement and remind ourselves of our intentions." I read the agreement, asked if we were all willing to keep it, and waited for nods. This was enough to get Patricia to think about her behavior and stop the disruption so the lesson could continue with everyone's attention, including hers. (Eventually, it gets so all I have to do is walk in the direction of the agreement, and students know they are being invited to keep it without my having to read it or say anything. We continue with the lesson undisturbed.)

Using the situation of Patricia and me as an illustration: If this had not been enough to end the disruption, I might continue the lesson as best I can. When students have enough information to get involved in their own exploration or discussion of the topic, I might walk over to Patricia and let her know we have a problem (this is done in the context of my having made a commitment to be constructive). I would invite her to think privately about what part or parts of the agreement she was not keeping. In Patricia's case, she might have said she wasn't listening, she wasn't being polite, she wasn't paying attention, she was disturbing others, and she wasn't acting with maturity. I also would ask if there is part of the agreement she thinks I am not keeping and honestly give her a chance to think about this and respond (perhaps I am talking too fast, or not giving enough time for questions). I would ask if she is willing to keep the agreement. Patricia, and most students I have found, would quite readily say yes by this time. Once she says yes, we are ready to move on. This takes from about forty seconds to two minutes and makes a huge difference when we reconvene as a group to hear what the rest of the class has experienced in their exploration/discussion and to continue with Patricia actively and cooperatively participating.

You may be thinking that it is highly unusual for a student willingly to state the negative things they are doing, admit to them, and then agree not to do them. It is the context in which this is all set up that makes the difference (see Chapter 1). Students deny responsibility when they know that admission will result in punishment. The type of "confrontation" I had with Patricia, however, is done in an atmosphere of trust, cooperation, and restoration and with the clear intention of "making things right" between us. This means that we knew that whatever happened, it would be reasonable, respectful, and restorative. I have assured my classroom community of this and invited them to tell me if I am not keeping this agreement. There is no need to hide what has happened because the intent is to be responsible and accountable and to move ahead when that occurs.

Another experience utilizing the respect agreement reminder involved John. After giving an assignment and time to work on it in class, John, instead of getting started on the assignment, was running up to people, acting like he was going to karate chop them, and actually hitting them once in a while. I asked him privately if he would be willing to read the respect agreement to himself and to think about which things on the agreement he was not keeping. He said he would. After he read them, we talked a little about what he identified as not keeping the agreement. He decided he was not treating others the way he would want to be treated, he was not being polite and nice, he was not getting his work done without disturbing others, and he was not acting in a way that would enable him to be prepared. I asked if he was still willing to keep the agreement that he had signed. He said he was. He got himself started on the assignment.

John needed a couple of additional reminders that were very brief when the same situation arose again. I would say, "John, are you remembering our agreement?" He would say, "Oh, yeah," and get to work. As the behavior stopped and as he kept our agreement, it became easier to trust him. I was not worried that he might hurt someone. I no longer felt I needed to watch him as carefully. I could relax and use the time students were working to walk around and help where help was needed, to correct a few papers, or to prepare for the next thing on the schedule.

As illustrated in this example, I try very hard to take action on my first observation of misbehavior because the sooner it is addressed, the better the chances are for restoring a respectful environment. This process is different from administering a punishment where I may give a number of warnings as I wait until the behavior becomes serious enough to deserve a punishment. The student's response is also very different as he or she enters into a problem-solving process with me rather than defending what he or she knows to be poor behavior in order to make the case for avoiding a punishment. An expectation of the standards develops a student's critical thinking ability, and following the Flowchart is a great way to meet this standard.

I do not view any of this as a waste of time; I view it as a positive way to reach and teach students the social curriculum. Students feeling they can trust a teacher to the point of being honest by recognizing what they are doing to keep themselves and others from learning maximizes the learning they will be able to do in the future. They learn to view these times as problem-solving opportunities rather than as times of "being in trouble." The more we connect and have positive experiences with making and keeping agreements (trust grows when agreements are made and kept), the more students take significant steps to changing in ways that will make a big difference in their behavior and decisions about learning. Part of the reason these changes make a big difference is ultimately they are making those changes themselves. If this is not enough to end a problem, I follow the map to the next stop on the Flowchart, which is to use active listening and/or an I-message. These will be discussed in the next chapter.

Chapter 5 • Active Listening and/or I-Message

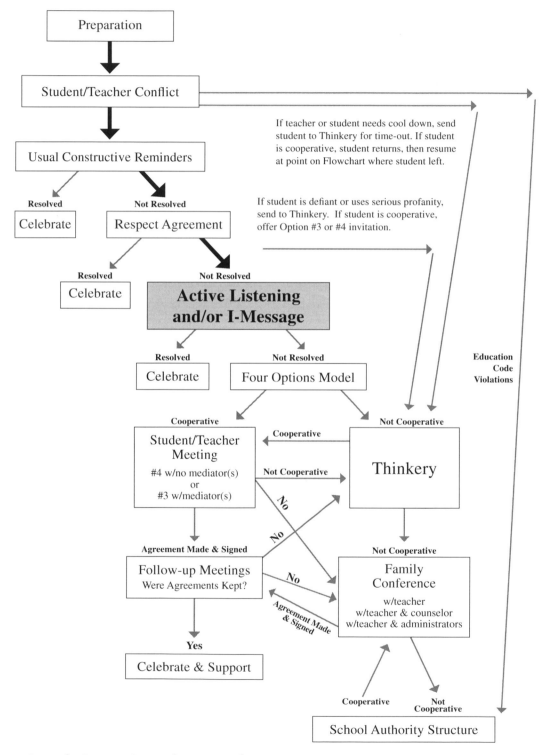

Preparation

Student/Teacher Conflict

If teacher or student needs cool down, send student to Thinkery for time-out. If student is cooperative, student returns, then resume at point on Flowchart where student left.

Usual Constructive Reminders

If student is defiant or uses serious profanity, send to Thinkery. If student is cooperative, offer Option #3 or #4 invitation.

Resolved — Celebrate

Not Resolved — Respect Agreement

Resolved — Celebrate

Not Resolved — **Active Listening and/or I-Message**

Resolved — Celebrate

Not Resolved — Four Options Model

Cooperative — Student/Teacher Meeting #4 w/no mediator(s) or #3 w/mediator(s)

Cooperative / **Not Cooperative** — Thinkery

Not Cooperative

Education Code Violations

Agreement Made & Signed — Follow-up Meetings Were Agreements Kept?

No / *No* / *No*

Not Cooperative — Family Conference w/teacher w/teacher & counselor w/teacher & administrators

Agreement Made & Signed

Yes — Celebrate & Support

Cooperative / **Not Cooperative**

School Authority Structure

Copyright © 2008 Ron and Roxanne Claassen

Chapter 5
Active Listening and I-Messages

Introduction

The formal Active Listening/I-Messages stop is rarely used with the 80% who are generally cooperative, occasionally used with the 15% who need more guidance and support, and most often used with the 5% who otherwise consume significant class instruction and teacher time almost daily. Active listening and I-messages are essential cooperation skills that are used not just at this stop on the Flowchart but also informally and frequently on many occasions and at every stop. This stop on the Flowchart is part of what we have referred to earlier as "constructive escalation" of a student/teacher conflict in order to gain the cooperation of students and their agreement to change/stop whatever behavior is causing the conflict. When one is at this point on the map, it means a student has refused to cooperate when usual constructive reminders have been offered. It also means they refused to keep the agreements they made concerning respect and ignored the friendly invitation to reconsider their commitment. It is time to be direct in letting the student know what you want by using an I-message or to listen to the student by using active listening skills if you think that approach is what they need.

Roxanne: A student who has arrived at school looking sad and distracted could benefit from active listening. Celia arrived at school one morning looking like she had been crying. Several of her friends were close around her trying to give her comfort. Once in the classroom, students took out their literature books to be ready for class. Celia sat down with nothing. I had been distracted with greeting students and gearing up for class. When I finally noticed Celia with nothing prepared, I tried the usual constructive reminders, which caused no change. I decided this was not a time for a respect agreement reminder and moved directly to active listening. It was obvious that something was really bothering Celia, rather than her being purposely disrespectful of herself or me. I quickly rearranged my lesson plan so I could get the rest of the class started on some individual seat work.

Celia and I went to one side of the room. She told me her grandmother was very sick, and her mother was thinking of leaving right away for Mexico. Celia was worried because the family knew it could be difficult for her mother to reenter the United States if she left suddenly. It was clear Celia needed some assurance about this situation before she could concentrate on her schoolwork. I arranged for Celia to talk with our superintendent, whom I knew would be better able to offer counsel to Celia's mother if she wanted it. Celia returned to class a half hour later feeling much better and ready to work.

A student who balks at learning new concepts in math by goofing off and not following the lesson could benefit from an I-message when the first stops on the Flowchart have not had any effect. Jorge became increasingly disruptive in math as the concepts became more and more complex. I had tried several usual reminders with little effect. I reminded him of his respect agreement commitment and that, too, had little effect. So then I approached him with an I-message. Following the pattern below, I said, "My purpose in talking to you is so you don't get lost and behind in math. I feel concerned when I am teaching a new concept and I notice that you are not paying attention or taking notes. My preference would be that you would be attentive and take notes and ask questions about anything you don't understand." He thought for a moment, got his book on the right page and began to participate by taking notes and asking a few questions.

Ron: I experience these two skills as the basic building blocks of conflict resolution and restorative justice. My personal experience in both using these two approaches (as a supervisor, teacher, and mediator), as well as in teaching them to others in graduate classes and seminars, reinforces that they are essential peacemaking skills. Following is my introduction to active listening and I-messages.

"What I learned when I 'tried out' active listening was that sometimes I hear but don't really listen." —a teacher

"When I think about it, the people I like to talk to are those who really listen." —a teacher

"I think the most outstanding characteristic about I-messages is that they are so respectful." —a teacher

"I had given him dirty looks, reprimanded him, sent him out of the room, and threatened him with a visit to the principal. Because of my assignment to 'try out' an I-message, I learned that I had never given him a clear, respectful message of what I wanted. When I finished he said, 'I could do that.' I am amazed at how effective it was." —a teacher

One reason control and coercive responses are utilized so much in schools to handle conflict or misbehavior situations is that teachers and administrators lack the essential skills required for cooperative problem solving.

The DTR Flowchart designates a special place for active listening and/or I-messages. This is because one or both of these skills is the DTR recommended response if a student has refused to respond constructively to the respect agreement reminder. However, while these skills are given special emphasis at this point on the Flowchart, they are actually utilized throughout the map. Without them, it would be impossible to implement Discipline That Restores.

These two skills are usually categorized as supportive (active listening) and assertive (I-messages). Listening is very closely related to caring and is obviously supportive. I-messages are effective in eliciting change and therefore are usually categorized as assertive. But it's also important to emphasize (and this will be demonstrated in the examples below) that active listening can be very assertive and I-messages, properly constructed, can be very supportive.

Both of these skills can be used for the life-giving purpose of utilizing cooperative processes to resolve conflicts and misbehaviors while building teacher/student relationships. It is also important to recognize that they also can be used to hurt and manipulate. This is why values, such as *respecting* and *deciding to be constructive*, must always be discussed when teaching these skills as prerequisites for their use.

There are many resources available that focus on teaching and providing guided experiences for practicing and utilizing these skills. Thomas Gordon, who wrote *Parent Effectiveness Training* and *Teacher Effectiveness Training*, introduced and emphasized both of these skills.

Active Listening

Active listening is an essential skill for peacemaking and conflict resolution because one of the things an upset student in a conflict wants is for the teacher to listen to his or her concerns. In the DTR Flowchart, one specific place where active listening might be utilized is when the teacher has reminded a misbehaving student of the respect agreement and the student has refused to respond or has actually said he or she won't keep it (which is very rare). Depending on the age and personality of the student, the teacher might do this with the whole class listening or in private, but never with the intent of embarrassing the student. The statement/question, an open invitation to tell why, has to be made in the context of the teacher's commitment to be constructive.

Teacher to student who has ignored or refused to cooperate after a respect agreement reminder: "You said you are refusing to keep the respect agreement?"

Most students will reconsider their decision regarding the respect agreement or will welcome the invitation to talk. If the student decides to talk, the teacher will soon be amazed by the new information gained that will be helpful in reestablishing the respect agreement.

Have you ever noticed that arguments get louder and louder? The reason for this is because each of the participants in the argument is subconsciously aware that the other is not listening. The false and subconscious hope is that by speaking louder, or shouting, the other will listen. You can observe this yourself if, when you find yourself in another argument with a student, teacher, or administrator, you can try out listening to what the other has to say and note the effect on the volume and tone. I think you will be amazed at what you observe. As you will see in the reflection below, you don't have to wait for an argument to try out the active listening skill. After introducing active listening and practicing it in class, I give the assignment to my students (administrators, teachers, and school counselors) to use consciously (try out) the skill, reflect on the experience, and write a short note summarizing it. We then share these in our next class. The following quote is based on a student's experience.

"On Tuesday morning I made a conscious effort to really listen when anybody spoke to me. I listened with my eyes, my facial expressions, with feedback, and body language. My children were first. When they talked to me, I stopped everything I was doing. I discovered that when I actively listened, they felt loved and were more content with themselves. I listened to their entire question before responding, and they were more accepting of my answers. There even seemed to be more harmony between them. When my husband talked, I let him continue until he was finished before I interjected my own thoughts. This was more difficult. I could tell he liked it. At school, I actively listened to any story, concern, or opinion that a student or teacher wanted to share. I felt really good. I felt more relaxed. Let me tell you, it was not always easy for me to let people finish what they were saying. Actually, I found that most people didn't even want my opinion; they just wanted me to listen. When I think about it, the people I like to talk to are those who really listen to me. I liked this exercise, and I am going to make a conscious effort to keep listening!"

Consciously trying out the active listening skill isn't an easy thing to do, and it's highly unlikely it will happen unless you have prepared yourself. In fact, even when you have prepared, it is likely that after an incident you will come to the recognition, "I could have tried listening." If you try it, you will find that it is welcomed by the other person. The person's voice volume will decrease, and, after he or she is sure you have listened, you will note that it seems very natural to invite changing the argument into problem solving. To try this out, of course, you need to know a few skills for listening and some strategies for constructive problem solving.

You will find that all constructive conflict management tools include listening. David Augsburger's *Caring Enough to Hear and Be Heard* is one source I have found very helpful. The following is adapted from his work:

1. Decide that you want to hear what the other has to say. This can be very hard when you disagree with what the other person is saying or if he or she has offended you. It is also true that you will be in a much better position to suggest something constructive if you know what the person wants, why the person wants it, or why he or she is doing something. It doesn't mean that you have a feeling of warmth for the person or that you are too weak to shout back. It means that you have decided to control yourself and that you have remembered your commitment to be constructive. Teachers are spoken to in a disrespectful way every day. Deciding to respond by listening requires discipline. ✳

2. Don't judge immediately. Try to understand what the person is saying from his or her point of view. Students come with reputations and often it is tempting to think, "I know why you are doing this." But just maybe we don't know. Listening first doesn't mean that you will never judge or evaluate what you are hearing. It means that you will first try to see it the way the student sees it and to feel it the way the student feels it. This requires some very conscious effort. You are in this incident or argument because each of you has different thoughts and feelings. It is tempting to think, "If the student would just see it the way I see it, then we wouldn't even be having this disagreement, conflict, or argument." To listen before judging means giving yourself permission to explore the possibility that just maybe there is another way of looking at it that is different from how you see it. It requires accepting the idea that you might not be the sole possessor of the truth. It just might be your truth, as you understand it, is not the whole truth.

3. Use nonverbal ways to let the person know you are open to hearing his or her thoughts and feelings. This is essential and very complex. It is essential because if our bodies tell the other person that we don't want to listen, the person won't tell us as much. For example, rubbing the back of your neck subconsciously conveys the meaning that what the other one is saying is a pain in the neck and you don't really want to hear it. This is complex because so much of it is done subconsciously. It is especially complex in cross-cultural situations. We all are part of several cultures. Part of what this means is that we know certain things that others of our same culture know without being told. It might include meanings attached to words, symbols, dress, etc. It also includes meanings attached to body movements or gestures. By definition, when you cross cultures, you don't know all of these meanings. So, the best we can do is to be authentic and honest in wanting to hear and to allow our bodies to convey this to the other person. If there is confusion, talk about the confusion. You just might have the great experience of learning a meaning from another culture.

4. Check to see if you have understood by summarizing or restating the other person's most important thoughts and feelings. Leave the focus on the other person. This is a serious attempt to find out if what you heard is what the person said or meant. It is important that you don't say anything in a tone that conveys that you know what the person has said better than the person does. Sometimes it happens that you did get the right words but the meaning that the speaker was trying to convey with those words didn't get through so the speaker might want to change the words. I start my summary with either no lead-in at all, or I use the short lead-in: "You said...?" Then, in my own words, I try to catch the meaning of the speaker's words and the accompanying feeling, when appropriate. Always use a tone that conveys that this statement is really a question. It is intended to invite the speaker to modify part or all of it or to confirm what I know so far, and it opens the door to go on and clarify or add to it. I prefer no lead-in or "You said...?" because the intent is to leave the focus on the speaker. I think that using a longer lead-in, such as, "What I think I heard you saying was...?" changes the focus from the speaker to me.

You might say, "This is just not me or my culture. I would never summarize like that." But I would challenge you to rethink this. I would suggest that all of us have used active listening. For example, if someone gives you detailed instructions on how to get somewhere you want to go, you probably summarize them to be sure you make the right turns at the right places. When someone tells us something that is very important to the speaker or to us, that is a good time to use the skill.

5. Don't advise, judge, analyze, bring up similar feelings, or ask questions. All these responses change the focus from the speaker to the listener. While these may be appropriate responses at other times, they're not when you want to listen. We often think that to get more information from another person we need to ask questions. This is certainly one option, but again it changes the focus from what the speaker wants to say to the area the listener wants the speaker to address. I have also found that by following the first four steps and resisting the temptation to respond in the ways listed above, I usually learn more than if I ask questions.

Because real active listening elicits more information and some at a deeper level, I feel the following is essential: *Please do not use these techniques with anyone unless you are unconditionally committed to being constructive with the person.* It is unethical to use this technique unless you will employ the resultant information for mutually constructive problem solving and efforts toward restoration and reconciliation.

Following are some more examples from teachers and administrators in my classes. Note how active listening is both a supportive and assertive activity.

Using active listening in a conflict with a student over a confiscated note:

> "It was disconcerting for me when I read the note. I decided this might
> be a time to *listen*. Instead of asking questions and trying to probe
> into the reasons why she had written the note, I just let the student
> talk. I restated things that she said and checked my understanding so
> that I was clear about what I had heard. It was amazing to me how

much this student revealed about herself while I listened. She disclosed many things that I am certain she would not have told me if she'd felt as if I was trying to elicit information from her. Because of this conversation, I am in a better position to help her work through some of the issues in her life that I would not otherwise have had the opportunity to do."

Using active listening while sitting on a school bus with a coworker:

"We began talking about our families. She shared some concerns and delights about her fourteen-year-old son. I immediately began to relate some things about my son at that age. The conversation was now about me, and she stopped talking. I felt bad. She tried again with another concern. This time I was determined to *listen*. I restated some of her thoughts and feelings, and she talked on and on. It felt really good to really be there to listen to her. I know our relationship is closer than before."

Using active listening while a husband tells about a bad banking experience (husband and wife had disagreed about which bank to approach first.):

"I could tell by the look on his face that he had something to tell me and that it was not good. I decided to *listen*. It was about the bank. I wanted to say 'See, we should have used my bank,' but I didn't. I decided to give him 100% of my attention, try to see it from his point of view, and check it out to see if I understood him. I didn't frown at him or show him any kind of disappointment. I truly listened to the situation and reminded myself of the times I had insisted on something and it hadn't turned out for the best. When he finished, we discussed some options and soon agreed on our next steps. He did not need my smart remarks about his choice in banks. He had already spent the day tormented over it. It was refreshing to have a touchy situation not become overheated, and I think he appreciated my constructiveness. I will definitely use this more often."

Using active listening with angry parent (parent arrives at school, is very agitated, and wants to speak with his son's teacher.):

> **Parent (to Teacher):** "My son says that you are always picking on him and making fun of him in front of the rest of the class. I think this is outrageous behavior for a teacher, and I'm going to ask to have my son transferred to another class."
>
> **Teacher to Parent** (remembering her commitment to be constructive): "Your son told you that I am treating him differently from the rest of the class, and that I am embarrassing him in front of his classmates. You are upset, and you won't allow your son to be in a class with a teacher who would act this way?"
>
> **Parent:** "That's right."
>
> **Teacher** (after a very brief explanation of the Four Options Model, next chapter): "How about if we use #4 to try to see if we can resolve this injustice in a way that is good for you, your son, and me? Are you willing to use #4?"
>
> **Parent:** "Okay, let's try it."

I mentioned before that while I consider active listening primarily as a supportive skill, it is also an assertive skill. I think it belongs in both categories. While it is clear why it belongs on the supportive side, it might not be quite as clear why it belongs on the assertive side. The reasons I think it also belongs on the assertive side are: 1) when one truly listens, the one speaking wants to tell more, and 2) when one truly listens, the other party is more likely to be open to cooperative problem solving. By listening, therefore, the listener is taking an assertive approach to problem solving. I don't think there is any more effective way to invite someone who is upset into a cooperative problem-solving process than by listening. Using this skill, especially when combined with the Four Options Model (see chapter 6) is both an assertive and supportive way of creating a context for constructive and cooperative problem solving.

At training events, I often have people work in small groups of three or four, and I have one person tell about something that "bugs" her or him. For the first three minutes, I have the others interrupt the speaker with similar thoughts ("that reminds me of …"), give advice ("you should try to…"), judge ("that's not such a big deal…"), etc. The result is a noisy group and quite a lot of laughter. On the surface it appears fun. The next round I ask the group to follow these active listening rules:

1. Decide that you really want to hear what the other has to say.
2. Don't judge immediately. Try to understand what the person is saying from his or her point of view.
3. Use nonverbal ways to let the person know you are open to hearing her or his thoughts and feelings.
4. Check to see if you have understood by summarizing the other person's most important thoughts and feelings.

The groups invariably become quiet and often lean toward each other. Afterward, when I ask about their experiences, I find that in the second round the speaker told the others much more and at a deeper level, giving reasons and describing meaningful experiences related to the person's current thoughts and feelings. The speaker often says that he or she gained some new insights about the situation. The listeners often say that they had a hard time only summarizing because they still wanted to give advice and share similar experiences. They are often amazed when the speaker thanks them for listening and helping her or him gain new insights.

Active listening is one of the essential skills utilized throughout the DTR Process and given special emphasis at this stop on the DTR Flowchart. The other essential skill is using I-messages.

I–Messages

Understanding how to construct and use an I-message is another essential skill for peacemaking and conflict resolution. In the DTR Flowchart, one specific place where an I-message (an alternative to using active listening) might be utilized is when the teacher has reminded a misbehaving student of the respect agreement and the student has refused to respond or has actually said she or he won't keep it (which is very rare). Depending on the age and the personality of the student, the teacher might offer an I-message with the whole class listening or in private, but never with the intent of embarrassing the student. The I-message has to be made in the context of the teacher's commitment to be constructive. The teacher might say:

"My purpose in talking with you is to clarify and improve our relationship."

"I am confused and feel disappointed when you violate our class respect agreement (can also describe specific behavior) and ignore my reminder, because I thought we had an agreement to keep our respect agreement."

"I would prefer that you keep it without my reminding you and that, if you forget, you respond positively when I remind you."

It is likely that the student will respond with an "Okay," or "I can do that." Occasionally a student might say something like, "I have changed my mind," or perhaps just continues to refuse to respond. In either case, the next step in the DTR Flowchart would be to invite the student to consider the Four Options. An I-message is a respectful way for the teacher to give a clear and constructive message to a misbehaving student. While it assertively states the problem and preference of the teacher for resolving it, an I-message is also supportive in its statement of purpose and a preference (not a closed demand) that opens the door for further discussion.

I-messages are assertive statements that convey a strong concern such that the speaker takes responsibility for what is said and invites the listener to consider the perspective of the speaker along with his or her own perspective. Many I-messages are short phrases such as, *I feel frustrated*, rather than saying, *You make me mad.* But often they are more complex.

I-messages, as in the short example above, are often contrasted with You-messages. You-messages, such as, "You are not keeping the respect agreement," are often experienced as "fighting words." You-messages are usually responded to by the listener with another You-message. In this case, the student might say, "You always pick on me!" A You-message usually escalates a conflict, whereas an I-message is received as a reasonable invitation to change or as an invitation to do problem solving.

From a teacher to a student who is out of his seat when the teacher is trying to start a lesson, a You-message:

"You never follow instructions. You know better than to be up walking around when I am starting a lesson. You have a detention."

The student may say something like this, a You-message:

"You never say anything when _____ is out of her seat. You're not fair."
And the student might think or even verbalize, "You are a _____."

An alternative for the teacher might be something like this, an I-message:

"I am saying this to you because I want you to be a successful learner and for me to be a successful teacher."
"I get distracted and feel frustrated when you are walking around while I am trying to start a new lesson."
"I'm afraid you will miss the content of the lesson or instructions for homework, and when I am distracted I am afraid I won't give adequate instruction to the others."
"I would prefer if you were at your seat and listening."

It is very likely that the student would say something like this, an I-message:

"I could do that," or "I needed to sharpen my pencil so I could write the instructions."

In either case, it is a constructive response that accepts responsibility rather than putting the responsibility on the teacher, as in the response to the You-message above. I-messages are usually responded to with more I-messages that either resolve the situation or provide additional information necessary for problem solving. I-messages can also suggest an alternative preference that might be acceptable or might lead to collaborative problem solving.

The I-message above follows a formula I use that is slightly modified from the way Thomas Gordon initially recommended. His formula included, "I feel (followed by naming the feeling one has when the problematic event occurs) when (a description of the event or activity that is problematic) because (followed by a rationale for why the activity causes the feelings)." I have observed that sometimes, unless the *purpose* is clarified for making this statement and a *preference* is stated for an alternate activity, the listener is left wondering, "Why are you telling me this?" or "Where are we headed with this?" I have found it most effective when I include my *purpose* as part of the statement and conclude the statement with my *preference*.

After I provide instruction and practice on I-messages in my seminars, I give the assignment to try out the skill (using the formula below), write up the experience, and evaluate the result. The participants bring these to the next class session and share them. Below is the formula used, followed by a few experiences.

My purpose is ... *(state relational constructive hope, goal, etc.)*

_____

_____

I feel and/or think ... *(state feelings and/or thoughts when the problem activity occurs)*

_____

_____

...when ... *(describe the problem activity)*

_____

_____

... because ... *(describe the reason that the activity is a problem for you)*

_____

_____

And, my preference would be... *(state one or two options that you think might resolve the problem activity; one option could be to invite the other to do some mutual problem solving with you).*

_____

_____

Teacher, a single mother, with college-aged son living at home:

> "**My purpose** in talking with you is to attempt to reduce the tension between us and to reduce our recently increasing confrontations. **I feel** frustrated and angry **and think** you don't care about me **when** I get up in the morning and find your dirty dishes in the sink and your clothes strewn around the house, **because** I have worked hard after getting

home from work to clean up the house, get dinner on, and clean up the dishes. **I would prefer** that you clean up after yourself so that the house is as clean in the morning as I left it when I went to bed." The mother said that her son listened, thought for a minute, and then responded, "I could do that."

High school teacher with a student failing a class:

"**My purpose** in talking with you is that I am concerned about your current grade. **I feel** scared and sad that you may not graduate **when** you do not come to school or stay focused in class **because** the time for reviewing in class right now is so important. **My preference** would be for you to come in on Monday and Tuesday during lunch and review for the final with me." The student agreed, and with no objections came in for the entire lunch periods. The teacher thinks he will pass.

Teacher (mother) who had yelled at her daughter when the daughter had started talking back and being uncooperative:

"**My purpose** in talking with you is to recognize our tension and try to help us improve our relationship. **I feel** frustrated and irritated and **I think** you hate me **when you** do not listen, **because** I would like you to pay attention to me as I speak to you without protesting. **I would prefer** that you listen to what I have to say before you begin your rebuttal and if you disagree with me, I am more than willing to use #4 to work it out." The daughter said she was sorry and then began to tell the mother about some problems she was having. Things became better between them.

Teacher with high school student:

"After being introduced to the I-message skill, I was eager to try it out with a student who had a habit of using foul language in class. Each time I had confronted him in the past, it seemed to get worse. I wrote out what I was going to say and the next morning after our class, I explained to him that I was taking a class and had an assignment to try out a new skill called an I-message. He agreed to participate with me. This is what I had written and then read to him:

"'**My purpose** in talking to you this morning is to discuss what can be done to improve our relationship. **I feel** very offended by your language and **I think** that you don't respect me or your classmates when you speak this way. I hear you swear and I immediately cringe, **because** I am your teacher and it makes me look bad to my other students when you don't stop swearing when I ask you to stop. **I would prefer** that you not use profanity at all, but at least not in class.'

"He looked at me, thought a minute, and simply replied, 'Okay.' This had really been bothering me for a long time. I had given him dirty looks, reprimanded him, sent him out of the room, threatened him with a visit to the principal, and now, because of this assignment, I discovered that all I needed to do was use this simple approach. I think it will also help him be more successful in school. Since our little experiment, although he has slipped a few times, he has stopped himself from swearing and looks at me for my approval and celebration of him keeping our agreement. I make a point of thanking him each time he catches himself. I think this might just stick!"

Teacher with another teacher:

"I am the person designated for facilitating special education meetings (IEPs). The teacher with whom I practiced this [I-message] is a special day class teacher. We meet together to schedule the upcoming meetings for her students. The problem is that she is supposed to pay attention to when the student meetings are due and contact me to schedule them. Because she doesn't remind me at all or she does it on the day a meeting is due, we end up in a panic trying to get the meeting set up so we won't be out of compliance. Then I find myself resenting her and having 'evil thoughts' about what I would say to her, something like, 'It's part of your job to remember this—not mine!' So, when I was given the assignment to try out the I-message, I decided this would be a good situation. I asked her if we could talk about it and told her I had an assignment that I hoped it would help us (purpose). I said, 'I feel stressed when we have to schedule our meetings at the last minute because I am worried that the parent won't be able to make it and we will be out of compliance. I would prefer if we could sit down together and figure out some kind of plan to take care of this.' Her response was, 'Sure, when do you want to get together?' I felt a whole lot better immediately, and I am hopeful that we can work it out."

Roxanne and I find these stories inspiring and encouraging. Our personal experience is that when we consciously utilize one or both of these skills, the outcome is always better than if we hadn't.

Our hope is that you will try out the skills. One great way is to say to the other person, "I have been reading this book, and it makes an assignment. I'm wondering if you would be willing to help me do my assignment?"

This chapter has focused on the two skills that we think are essential to implement constructive conflict resolution and restorative justice. As we said at the beginning of the chapter, while these skills are separate stops on the DTR Flowchart, we want to also emphasize that they are utilized throughout the Flowchart.

If a student has refused several invitations to cooperate and you have used your best speaking (I-messages) and listening (active listening) skills, a visual can be very helpful. The next chapter focuses on a visual that is central to this whole concept of Discipline That Restores. It provides another way to offer an invitation to cooperate—the Four Options Model.

Chapter 6 • **Four Options Model**

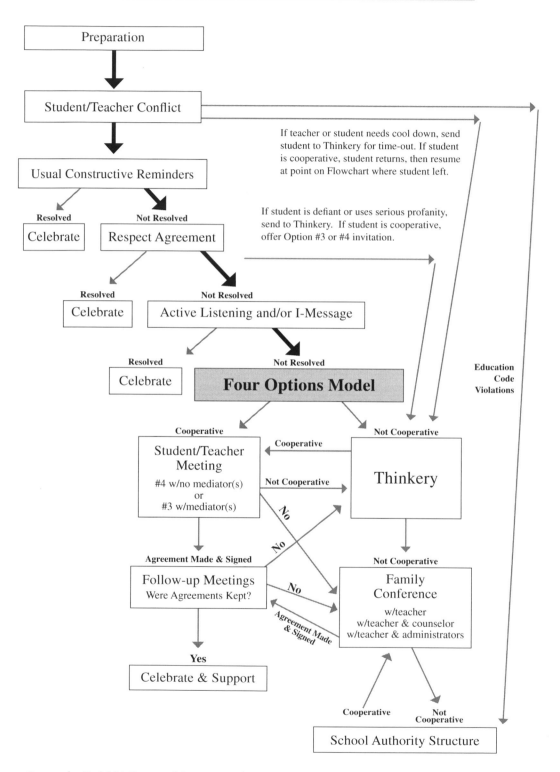

Copyright © 2008 Ron and Roxanne Claassen

Chapter 6
Four Options Model

"Like all brilliant things in life, [the Four Options Model] is elegant, simple, and unfortunately, not well enough known. We need to spread it out. When people begin to grasp its significance, it will be even more powerful. It has the power to transform our society."

Doug Noll
Attorney/Mediator/Educator
Board Chair, San Joaquin College of Law

Introduction

DTR is not permissive in that it does not allow a student's bad behavior to disrupt the learning environment, and it also does not give up quickly on the idea of cooperation. Roxanne says that this model provides an invitation that is incredibly respectful yet powerful. She says, "It is amazingly simple yet deep and effective. I really can't imagine how teachers or other leaders can work effectively without it."

At this stop on the Flowchart (fortunately only a few students reach this point), the conflict/disrespect/power struggle has escalated because the student has refused several invitations to cooperate. The student has refused to modify his or her behavior after usual constructive reminders, a respect agreement reminder, and invitations to cooperate using I-messages and/or active listening. At this point, the dangers in the conflict are apparent and the opportunities seem remote. The teacher is tempted to take a punitive action. This is another place where it is helpful to remember one's commitment to be constructive and that all misbehavior provides teaching opportunities. All of these

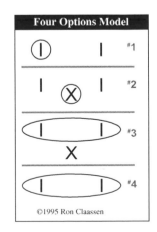

73

reminders and invitations have been designed to encourage students to self-monitor their behavior and act in ways that are respectful, civil, and cooperative. The Four Options Model is an invitation to cooperate that also requires the student to think consciously about the alternatives to non-cooperation.

After reading this chapter, you will recognize that each of these reminders is an invitation to the student to change from doing #1 (power over) to #4 or #3 (power with). Each reminder escalates the caring confrontation, always with the intent of using the least possible outside force to help the student reconsider behavior and choose a constructive and cooperative track with the class and teacher. If the student has refused to modify the off-task, disruptive, and/or disrespectful behavior (all #1's) based on the reminders/invitation, the teacher continues the constructive and caring confrontation by using the Four Options Model to invite the student to join with the teacher in problem solving. It might sound something like this: "Darren, it seems that we have a conflict and, as you know, we will use one of our four options [see figure]. You know I would prefer #4 [pointing to #4 if using a small model]. Which would you prefer?" Notice that the choice given to the student is not whether we will address the problem, but which option we will use to address the problem. The Four Options Model is a tool a teacher can use to help the student understand the options both visually and verbally. Teachers who have learned to use the Four Options Model find it to be a very effective tool.

Not everyone is inclined to use a visual model. But even those who aren't find the Four Options Model helpful. Roxanne says, "Using a model does not come naturally to me. However, I found it so helpful that I wanted to use it. Now I can't imagine doing without it. It has become a natural response for me. I bring a student's attention to the model and invite her or him to join me in #4. The student almost always does. It only takes a few seconds for this amazingly complex transaction. Once a student agrees to #4, the off-task, disruptive, or disrespectful behavior stops—not because I made him or her stop, but because the student has chosen to do cooperative problem solving with me. It's almost too good to be true. Then we schedule a time to meet later."

Understanding the Model

Ron: I developed the model to help me understand a book I was reading, *Getting Disputes Resolved,* by Ury, Brett, and Goldberg of the Harvard Negotiation Project. I was first a math teacher (my BA and MA majors were in mathematics), and to me it is important to be able to draw a picture or model of complex concepts. The book suggested that there were just three ways to resolve conflict: power, rights, and interests. It was in trying to draw a picture of this concept that the Four Options Model emerged.

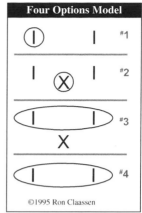

A model, like a mathematical formula or proof, is most helpful when it is simple yet represents a very big and complex reality. It has been said that you can tell if a model is valuable by noticing if people point to it as they talk and attempt to communicate. If a teacher extends the invitation with a copy of the model within reach of the student in addition to the verbal invitation, the student may not even have to say anything but can indicate that she or he has decided to cooperate by pointing to #4. A model makes it possible to communicate with fewer words and at the same time with greater clarity. A model can also help us think, analyze, and decide about something, often in new ways. A good model can be understood and utilized at many different levels of complexity. A good model stimulates dialogue, which often leads to new insights. My hope is that you will "try out" the model and that you will find it stimulating and helpful.

Understanding the Model: Definitions

It takes about one minute to gain a basic understanding of the Four Options Model (later referred to as just "model"); however, the nuances may take a lifetime to unpack. The model describes four basic response options and an infinite number of variations illustrated by "I"s, "X"s, circles or ovals and by the lines that separate them. While the model looks like it applies to just two-party conflicts, each "I" may represent any number of persons.

The "I"s represent the people in the conflict and/or the ones needing to make a decision.

The "X"s represent *outside* people (or perhaps outside objective criteria) who get involved but are not part of the conflict and who are not one of those who need or want to have a decision made.

The circle or oval is around the one(s) who have the ability (to make the decision or control the situation. The circle relates to power.

The lines between the options serve the purpose of helping clarify that when moving along the continuum between options there is a place where the decision maker(s) changes.

Understanding the Model: Illustrations and Interpretation

Option #1 is where one "I" (one of the parties in the conflict) has the ability to control the situation or make a decision that will have an effect on both. The "I" who is in the circle has the ability (for some reason) to control the situation or decision and the other "I" goes along. The ability to control the situation is often based on positional authority that may or may not be seen as giving legitimate authority to the "I" in the circle over the "I" outside the circle. For example, a teacher has been given authority over the students and the principal has authority over the teachers. Other factors influencing the ability of an "I" to control the situation or decision may, or may not, include a high degree of respect (the respected elder in the family), the ability to threaten and hurt another (a bully), age (older siblings), education (the teacher), a substantial physical size (adult with a small child) or verbal advantage (teacher with first-grade students), etc.

Other examples:

A police officer making an arrest.

A teacher giving a student a detention.

A parent telling a small child that he or she can't go outside.

A supervisor requiring an employee to change a procedure.

A firefighter clearing a building.

A person with a gun making demands.

If this option has been used, when a trusted person not involved in the conflict talks to the "I" who is not in the circle, the "I" outside the circle will say something like, "It was not my decision to make," "I had no choice," or "I had to go along." Sometimes the "I" outside the circle will be upset or even very angry; sometimes this "I" will be okay with the arrangement or even thankful. Both logical consequences and punishments happen at #1, but the difference between the two is that with logical consequences, the one outside the circle experiences the consequence as respectful, reasonable, restorative, and reintegrative.

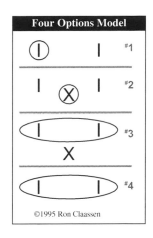

Option #2 is where the "X" (the outside party or objective criteria) makes a decision for the "I"s (the ones in the conflict or the ones needing to make a decision). The "X" may listen to the experiences, concerns, and preferences of the "I"s, but the decision is made by the "X." For example, a teacher might listen to two students who are having a conflict and make a decision about what should happen. Or, a teacher might listen to a teacher and a parent and student in a conflict situation and make a decision on what should happen. The "I"s may both like the decision or at least accept it. But sometimes one may like it and the other not like it, and sometimes both don't like it. Sometimes the "I"s have mutually chosen a trusted person to be the "X" and asked for a decision, and because of this are more accepting of the decision. Sometimes the "X" is an unknown to both parties. Sometimes one of the "I"s has chosen option #2 and the other has little or no say in the matter.

Other examples:

A court with judge or jury making the decision for the parties.

An arbitrator making the decision for the parties.

A wise and trusted elder making the decision in a family conflict.

A vice principal making the decision for two students.

Option #2 is used in the DTR Flowchart when a party in the conflict or violation situation has refused to use #3 or #4 or when the state or school rules require an authority to take an action. When DTR is in place and #2 is employed, the decision of the authority will be reasonable, respectful, restorative, and reintegrative.

Option #3 also includes an "X," meaning there is some outside involvement. The role of the "X" is to assist, in some way, the "I"s inside the oval to arrive at that point where they say they agree on the decision or the action to be taken. The role of the "X" may range from presence to very active involvement in both process and content. This role will be discussed more thoroughly in Chapter 7. An example of a #3 at school is when a teacher helps two students resolve a conflict but allows them to make the decision. Another example would be having students trained as mediators to help other students resolve conflicts. A formal program in schools is often referred to as a peer mediation program.

Other examples:

A professional mediator with two parties who make an agreement.

Student mediators helping other students.

A supervisor helping two employees decide how to solve a problem.

A mediator with a victim and offender who decide how to make things right between them.

The #3 option is used in the DTR Flowchart at the Student/Teacher Meeting or Family Conference if there is need for an outside person to lead the process.

If, in a safe setting, the "I"s say, "We didn't really make the decision. It was really made by the 'X,'" then it wasn't really a #3, it was a #2. Or, in a safe setting, if one of the parties says, "I didn't really have a choice because the 'X' teamed up with the other 'I' and they made the decision," then instead of the #3, it was really a #1 (the "X" and an "I" in one circle and the other "I" outside the circle). Or, in a safe setting, if one of the parties says, "I didn't really have a choice because the other 'I' was the one who made the decision," then it was a #1 with both the "I" and the "X" outside the circle. In a true Option #3, there is no decision made or action taken until the "I"s agree.

Options #3 and #4 are similar in some ways and yet different in other ways. They are similar in that the oval encircles both "I"s, so the decision resides with those inside the circle, and not with just one of them (as in Option #1) or with "X" (as in Option #2).

Option #4 does not include an "X," meaning the decision made or the action taken is something that is agreed on by the "I"s with no outside involvement. It may not be the first choice of one or the other or both, but it is something on which they voluntarily and cooperatively agreed. It does not mean that their power was equal (two parties never have equal power, and their power might not even be close), but it does mean that in a safe setting both would say, "Yes, I know that I had other options, but I decided to voluntarily go with our decision and we have an agreement." An example of this model in the classroom would be the teacher and student making an agreement about asking the teacher for help on homework that the student doesn't understand, rather than the student turning in a homework assignment that is not completed.

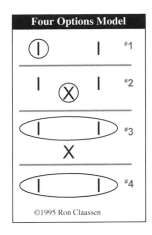

Other examples:

> Two people deciding on where to eat lunch together.
>
> Two employees deciding how to solve a problem together.
>
> A teacher and student deciding how to resolve tardy issues.
>
> An employee and a supervisor solving a problem together.

If in a safe setting, one or more of the "I"s says, "I really had no choice," or "I don't agree with the decision," then it wasn't really a #4, it was a #1. For example, students (and sometimes parents) are asked to sign behavior modification contracts devised by a teacher or administrator to allow the student to remain in class. Since the student would most likely say, "I had no choice and no part in developing the agreement," this would be a #1 rather than a #4. If the teacher or administrator wanted the contract to be a #4, the teacher or administrator would need to invite the student's participation in both the development of the agreement and the decision.

In the DTR Flowchart, all of the stops (Usual Constructive Reminders, Respect Agreement, I-messages and/or Active Listening) are invitations and reminders for the student who is off-task, misbehaving, or disrespectful to join the teacher in an informal #4. The Student/Teacher Meeting (Chapter 7) and the Family Conference (Chapter 10) are formal #4 invitations (or sometimes #3s).

We will now describe how the model is used as a tool in the classroom and then return to providing additional information about each option.

Using the Model as a Tool

Following the map of the DTR Flowchart, the Four Options Model is used (visual and verbal) because the student has refused to modify her or his behavior after the informal usual constructive reminders, a respect agreement reminder, and invitations to cooperate using I-messages and/or active listening. All of these reminders and invitations are designed to encourage the student to choose to join the teacher in a cooperative #4. As you can see, DTR is not permissive (it does not allow a student's bad behavior to disrupt the learning environment), and it does not give up quickly on the idea of cooperation. The DTR Flowchart provides a series of strategies designed to gain the cooperation of students by asking them to self-monitor their behavior. Each reminder escalates the caring confrontation, always with the intent of using the least possible outside force to help the student decide to get back on a constructive and cooperative track with the class and teacher.

The Four Options Model is a tool (verbal and visual) to help the teacher continue the constructive escalation while inviting the student to choose to cooperate. A teacher might say something like, "Sammy, we have a problem that we need to work on. As you know, I prefer #4 [pointing to the #4 option on a model] but I can't do that alone. I need to know if you are willing to join me in #4 or, if not, which option would be your preference." If Sammy says, "Yes, I also prefer #4" (as most students will), Sammy has indicated to his teacher that he is willing to search for a way of resolving the problem that is acceptable to both him and the teacher.

It is important at this point to pause and reflect on the amazingly complex transaction that has just happened. The model has been used after the student has refused several times to cooperate. Then, rather than this escalating into a power struggle followed up with punishment, the student and teacher have agreed to cooperate. And this amazingly complex transaction has taken place in the midst of a classroom of twenty to thirty students. It is especially amazing because it is all accomplished in just ten to thirty seconds, allowing the teacher to return quickly to the planned curriculum. It is also important to note that the teacher did this while feeling disrespected and despite a "gut" desire to send the student out of the room for punishment. Instead, because of a commitment to being constructive and by following the Flowchart, the teacher has utilized the model as another tool to invite cooperation, even when emotions are escalated. (My dissertation research indicates that teachers feel less stress knowing that they have this option to fall back on when the student has not responded to the other reminders and invitations. My research also indicates that teachers regard themselves as more effective leaders when they use the model in the midst of a conflict.) By using the model, in less than thirty seconds, roles (determining who will make the decision) and intent (looking for an agreement that is mutually satisfactory) have been clarified. Using the model substantially reduces the teacher's likelihood of reacting defensively. The climate for both participants (and the class) is very different than when the teacher uses a #1 (without clarifying what he or she is doing). Rather than an open power struggle and the danger side of conflict, the teacher has created another learning opportunity for the misbehaving student and avoided a major disruption to the entire class.

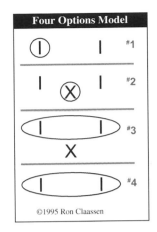

When Sammy indicates that he is willing to do #4 with the teacher, he will almost always immediately modify his off-task, disruptive or disrespectful behavior. This does not mean that the problem is solved. The model was used because frequent other reminders did not resolve the problem. The model itself is not designed to solve the problem but to determine what process will be used to address the problem so that it can be resolved. Once the teacher has decided to offer the model and if the student agrees to work at #4, it is very important that the teacher follows through and has a Teacher/Student Meeting (see Chapter 7), the next stop on the DTR Flowchart. Even though the student usually modifies the immediate bad behavior, the problem is likely to reoccur if an agreement is not developed to address it long term. If it was the first time Sammy refused to respond to the reminders, then it might be that he would offer a quick and verbal affirmation of his earlier agreement to abide by the Respect Agreement. In this case, the Teacher/Student Meeting might be very quick and informal, and the teacher might decide not to have a special meeting. But if it has happened repeatedly, there is a lack of trust issue between Sammy and the teacher due to a lack of agreements or agreements being made and not kept. When in doubt about whether or not a formal written agreement is necessary, go ahead and write an agreement. A written agreement is always helpful.

The Teacher/Student Meeting provides an opportunity to clarify and renew agreements or make new ones. Using this as an occasion to make agreements is important because *it is when people make and keep agreements that trust grows.* If Sammy and the teacher are unwilling to make agreements or make them and then don't keep them, trust will diminish. You can count on it. There is no magic to trust building. It is very predictable.

If Sammy refuses the invitation to do #4 (which is rare) but chooses #3, then the teacher should welcome and honor this choice. If Sammy chose #3, he will most likely modify his immediate bad behavior and further discussion of it could wait for the meeting. The next step would be to decide together with Sammy who among the trained mediators on the campus would be acceptable to both of them. The teacher would then take the initiative to arrange for the mediator, who would meet with each of them individually to prepare for the mediation and then arrange a meeting time and place.

If Sammy refuses both #4 and #3 or chooses #1 or #2, it would be a good time to do some active listening and teaching if needed to be sure he understands what he is choosing. DTR does not give in to bad behavior and does not give up quickly on the idea of cooperation. It may be that he doesn't understand the options. This is a teaching opportunity to help him understand the options and who makes the decision in each. If time or circumstances (thirty other students wanting attention) do not permit such a discussion, the other alternative on the DTR Flowchart map would be to refer Sammy to the Thinkery (Chapter 9). The purpose of referring Sammy to the Thinkery would be to help him understand his choices so far, to think about why he made those choices, to consider the impact of those choices on him and others, and to reconsider if he might really want to cooperate and do #4 or #3. The Thinkery is not to punish Sammy but to help Sammy remember and clarify his goals, to make responsible choices, and to cooperate in problem solving. It may be that when Sammy is out of the class and with a person who has helped him calm down and think more rationally, he will change his mind and choose to return to the class with an offer to cooperate and do #3 or #4.

It is possible that Sammy will choose #2 because he does not trust that his teacher would really do a #4. It might be that in his experience, adults always do #1, even when they make the words sound like they are willing to do #4. In that case, the person in the Thinkery might encourage him to try a #4 and give his teacher a chance. If this doesn't feel safe to him, the Thinkery person would encourage him to at least try a #3, with a person he trusts as the "X." Over time and with consistent experiences with his teacher, Sammy will gain confidence that they really can do a #4.

It also might be that Sammy refuses #3 or #4 because he has done it before and realizes the level of responsibility and accountability required. He may prefer to have the teacher punish him, since, in his experience, punishment does not require one to accept responsibility or to make any changes for the future. Roxanne's experience is that when this happens, as it does occasionally, the student usually will change her or his mind if invited to discuss the reasons for wanting the punishment. If this does not change a student's mind, Roxanne will often invite the student's parents to join them in their decision-making at a Family Conference (Chapter 10). When parents become aware of the options that have been offered to cooperate, they advise (sometimes with significant intensity) their child to try out a cooperative process, #3 or #4.

> **Ed Barton, school counselor/mediator**: "I think that showing the Four Options Model increases cooperation. First of all, they get to see that there are several options. It gives them a view of the end result. Either they are going to participate in the decision or they are going to have someone else make the decision. Looking at the visual gives them a much better picture of the options and what will happen if they don't cooperate."

It is very important to remember that the purpose of using the model is not to solve the problem but to help decide which process will be used to address the problem. It is essential that the student is offered the options and makes a choice. If this conscious choosing of an option is left out and a teacher tries to *make* the student participate in a cooperative problem-solving process, it will probably really be a #1. Cooperative problem solving requires all parties to decide voluntarily to cooperate. If the student doesn't clarify this choice, the level of acceptance of responsibility will be diminished. It is possible that the student will refuse the invitations to #4 or #3 and prefer #2, a decision by an authority. This choice and decision make it more likely the student will accept the decision (see Chapter 11).

Another value in using the model is to help the teacher continue teaching rather than becoming defensive or reactive. It would be common for a teacher confronted with a student who has refused the earlier invitations to react with anger and just do a #1 (give a detention, take away a privilege, embarrass or intimidate the student in front of the class, etc.). The model is a tool to give the teacher a reliable and rational structure to follow so that anger and coercion are not the only options for responding to the situation. For a teacher, the model becomes a trusted tool, even for people like Roxanne who are not naturally attracted to models.

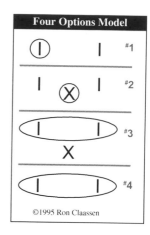

Roxanne, eighth-grade teacher: "The visual is very important. The Four Options Model provides another strategy for inviting the cooperation that we need to be a community. When students have refused several invitations to cooperate, the model is a tool for getting the focus off of how mad we are at the other and getting the focus onto something that is between us, and then seeing so clearly what our options are. The model is amazingly simple yet deep and effective. I really can't imagine how teachers or other leaders can work effectively without it."

Chapter 7 • **Student/Teacher Meeting**

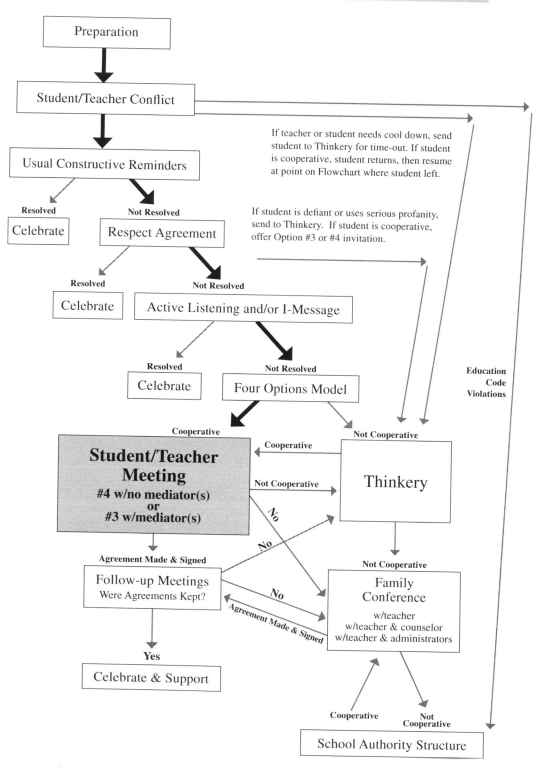

Preparation

Student/Teacher Conflict

If teacher or student needs cool down, send student to Thinkery for time-out. If student is cooperative, student returns, then resume at point on Flowchart where student left.

Usual Constructive Reminders

Resolved — Celebrate

Not Resolved — Respect Agreement

If student is defiant or uses serious profanity, send to Thinkery. If student is cooperative, offer Option #3 or #4 invitation.

Resolved — Celebrate

Not Resolved — Active Listening and/or I-Message

Resolved — Celebrate

Not Resolved — Four Options Model

Education Code Violations

Cooperative / **Not Cooperative**

Student/Teacher Meeting #4 w/no mediator(s) or #3 w/mediator(s)

Cooperative — (to Student/Teacher Meeting)

Not Cooperative — Thinkery

Thinkery — **Not Cooperative**

Agreement Made & Signed — Follow-up Meetings — Were Agreements Kept?

No ... *No* ... *No* ... Agreement Made & Signed

Family Conference w/teacher w/teacher & counselor w/teacher & administrators

Yes — Celebrate & Support

Cooperative / **Not Cooperative**

School Authority Structure

Copyright © 2008 Ron and Roxanne Claassen

Chapter 7
Student/Teacher Meeting

Trust grows when agreements are made and kept, and trust diminishes if we are unwilling to make agreements or if agreements are made and not kept. – Ron Claassen

Part 1

Introduction, Examples, and Reflections on Using the Student/Teacher Meeting Process

When a student has been disruptive and disrespectful and has rejected numerous invitations to cooperate, and when you, the teacher, and that student have agreed to use Option #4, the student/teacher meeting is a reliable process to help you and the student recognize the violations, restore equity between you, and for you both to create a plan for a better future. Due to the escalation of the conflict, the meeting requires more than just an informal conversation. This chapter provides an introduction, examples, and reflections on using the process (Part 1), the theory behind it (Part 2), and the details of the strategy (Part 3) to help lead a student /teacher meeting successfully. The chapter concludes with stories of student/teacher meetings (Part 4) and an agreement form with instructions on how to use it (Part 5).

As you see the formality and the strategy involved, remember that you will use this only occasionally with the most difficult students. This chapter emphasizes theory and specific strategies, not because you use it more frequently, but because when you do need it, you are working with a student who has refused several invitations to cooperate, already indicating a situation that is more complex and requires increasing the formality to match the complexity.

The process that follows will most likely seem unfamiliar because it is in a step-by-step format. However, this is simply putting into a step-by-step strategy the process that people describe when telling about moving from hurt and violation to making peace. The reason for including this detail is to help the teacher work constructively with the 5% of students who do not respond to informal reminders to cooperate. (And, by the way, these students will not modify their behavior when punishment is administered.) Roxanne has found that this process works very well with the most difficult students.

You will note in this step on the Flowchart, that Option #3 is another possibility for this Student/Teacher Meeting. Sometimes, due to the complexity of the situation or the intensity you feel, you or the student may decide to use Option #3. That would mean that you would invite a mediator to lead your Student/Teacher Meeting while still following the strategy outlined below.

The Student/Teacher Meeting stop on the Flowchart is an opportunity to give misbehaving, off-task students the chance to get the attention they need in order to get back on task so their learning is not interrupted and they are not interrupting the learning of others. It is helpful to remind oneself that this is a teaching opportunity that can make a big difference in the habits of the child. Working on the problem will also make a difference for the teacher and the comfort he or she feels in the classroom community. The other students will also experience more comfort. Students who are on task do not like constant interruption and misbehavior by a few. They appreciate it when the teacher takes a leadership role in getting such things resolved. The leadership that teachers provide puts the responsibility on the person who is misbehaving and invites that person to be accountable.

These meetings can range in length. The less time that elapses between the bad behavior and the deciding with the student to work on the problem, the less time the meeting needs to take, because there is not a lot of built-up anger and/or a huge collection of injustices. This Student/Teacher Meeting can be accomplished during a fifteen-minute break. If the problem has been going on for a time, the meeting will take longer. Longer meetings will need a lunch period or an hour after school. They can be done in more than one session if time is difficult to find. Students can usually remember very well what happened in the earlier meeting and can make agreements to stop something in the interim if the meeting cannot be completed in a single session. In either case, make sure such meetings end with a written agreement that is clear about what is going to be done to solve the problem. Both teacher and student sign the agreement, and a follow-up meeting (time, date, location) is arranged. As we look at an actual situation, Roxanne will give you a better idea of what a student/teacher meeting includes. As you will note, a meeting like this takes some time. All discipline plans take time. Roxanne prefers using her time this way because most of the time spent is learning time.

A Student/Teacher Meeting Story

Roxanne: I will illustrate the flow of a student/teacher meeting by telling the story of one such meeting. When I give homework, I do not always collect it and correct it. I walk around the room before class begins to see if each person has completed homework. As I came to Roberta, I could see that she was frantically copying Monica's algebra homework. This was not the first time she had not had her homework and now there was the added issue of copying. I leaned in to talk to the girls as privately as I could. I let them know that we had a problem (they were well aware of this). I nodded in the direction of the Four Options Chart that hangs beside our respect agreement and asked them which option they wanted to use to solve our problem, since it was a pretty big problem that we had already tried to solve informally. They wanted to use Option #4. I let them know that I thought this was great. We decided to meet during lunch. In the meantime, Monica took back her paper, and Roberta took a zero for homework that day. I let them know we would decide formally what should happen at our meeting.

This part of the intervention was not disruptive to the rest of the class and took about three minutes, less time than it would have taken me to fill out two detention forms and calling each parent. Then I would also have needed to follow up with a form letter to the parents so the school and I would have a written record that parents had been contacted. I would need to get the detention turned in to the dean of students, and he would need to schedule it, make sure the students served it, monitor them while they were there, and then inform me of the completion of the punishment. This does not even include the possible power struggle I would have now entered with each of these students if they thought this was somehow unfair, went home, and gave a less than complimentary version of how it was all handled to their parents. Students sometimes go home and emphasize that this happened to them in front of everyone and that it embarrassed them hugely, while deemphasizing their actual wrongdoing. When this type of punitive discipline happens, meetings may be called, but they do not begin in a positive atmosphere. Rather, the teacher is often the one on the defensive.

Roberta, Monica, and I met at lunch. I showed the girls where we were on the Flowchart and thanked them for being willing to work on the problem. It was now time to look at another model. I took out the Peacemaking Process (Part 3) and reminded them of the process we would use to work together and made sure we were all there to be constructive and willing to solve the problem. They were familiar with this because I had spend the first several weeks of social studies teaching the entire class the strategies for peacemaking (I use the *Making Things Right* curriculum written by Ron and me, available at amazon.com or disciplinethatrestores.org).

We started by assuring each other that we would be constructive (Step 1) and would abide by the ground rules (Step 2), which included checking with the girls to make sure it was all right with them for me to lead the meeting. We continued with Step 3 by describing, recognizing, and summarizing the injustice(s) as described on the Yellow Card (this is a 3 × 5 card with the Four Options Model on one side and an abbreviated version of A Peacemaking Process, on the other; see page 101 or disciplinethatrestores. org). I asked Roberta to describe how she experienced the conflict and to include both facts and feelings. We would decide as we went who should summarize, Monica or me. Roberta began by saying she did not get her homework done because she had not taken her book home. She thought she would do it during other class time but that had not worked out. I summarized this part of her story. She went on to say she was bothered because she knew there was at least one other time she had not done her homework, and she did not like getting a zero. She begged and pleaded with Monica to let her copy her homework. Monica had not been sure she wanted to do this, but Roberta said she had put a lot of pressure on her, calling her a "goody-goody" and threatening her with not being her friend. Monica summarized this part. I asked if Roberta wanted to say anything else about what had happened or how she felt about it. She said she just felt really awful, especially because she had broken the respect agreement and she knew she had caused Monica to break it as well. I summarized this. She went on to say how worried she was about her grade and what another zero might mean. I also summarized this.

I turned to Monica and asked her to say how she had experienced the situation. Monica said that when it was time to take out homework to be checked, Roberta told her she did not have hers and asked Monica for her paper so she wouldn't get another zero. Monica did not want to let this happen. Roberta promised never to ask her again, but said that it was really important to her this time because she had not understood what she was supposed to do. Roberta summarized this part of Monica's experience. Monica went on to say she had again said no, but then Roberta called her a "goody-goody." She finally gave in when she thought Roberta would not be her friend (acceptance by the girls was very important since only nine of the thirty-one students in this class of eighth graders were girls). I summarized this part of her experience and asked her if there was more she wanted to say. She said she was really embarrassed by the situation because she knows allowing someone to cheat is wrong, but it didn't seem so bad since it was just homework. I summarized and asked again if either girl wanted to say anything else.

Now it was my turn to say how I experienced the problem. I began by saying how surprised I was to see that Roberta was copying Monica's homework, since I know both of them to be good students who like to do their own work. I also knew Roberta had not gotten all of her homework assignments done previously and felt in the pit of my stomach that we needed to do something about this. I did not want anyone to think that cheating was a good way to learn. I asked Roberta to summarize this. I went on to say that I could see that Monica was very uncomfortable and embarrassed to be in this situation, and yet I could see that she had allowed Roberta to use her paper. I told them I was disappointed when something like that happens, because I know it is not possible for someone to learn new concepts themselves if they do not practice on their own. Monica and Roberta both summarized this. I told them I did not have anything further to add and asked them once more if they had anything else they wanted to say. Both said they were sorry at the same time.

I acknowledged their apologies by smiling and saying that was very helpful and part of Step 4, Restoring the Equity and Clarifying Future Intentions. I explained that we needed to restore balance to our relationship now. Their apologies helped a lot because the girls let me know that they knew what they had done was wrong and they were willing to take responsibility. I also said that it is sometimes helpful to work on restoring equity and clarifying future intentions at the same time. Step 4 includes inviting us to think about what agreements are needed in order to clarify the future so that we do not have to worry about something like this happening again. I took out paper for each of us to write our ideas separately. I reminded us that all suggestions would be subject to the guidelines asking that whatever we do, it should be related, reasonable, respectful, and restorative. We each began thinking and writing.

When each of us finished writing, we read the suggestions out loud. I put them on chart paper so we could look at the ideas all at once. Now, there is rarely anything earth-shattering about what the suggestions are, and, even though they are often obvious, the value in all of this is that we have been intentional about what could be done. This makes a difference in whether what we thought we should do is actually done. The ideas were: be sure to take home the books needed for homework; do your own work; get help ahead of time if there is something you don't understand; don't ask a friend to do something you know is wrong; be willing to help but unwilling to cheat; don't cheat; apologize; and then, don't do it again. Next we needed to look at the list and decide what things we would be willing to do to solve the problem. We decided all were reasonable, related, and restorative and that most of the ideas were future oriented. Monica and Roberta wanted to do all of the ideas, which was fine with me.

We still needed to figure out how to balance things right now. The apologies were helpful, but what about the missed assignment? What about Monica? Should she do something beyond the apology? What about me? Was there something I needed to do? Immediately Roberta asked if she could have one more day to complete the assignment. She thought it was reasonable that she not get full credit but wondered if she could have some credit. I let her know that I thought this was a good idea. I told her the purpose of homework was to help students be better able to understand concepts and that I really had no problem giving her full credit if she did the work herself. I asked her if it were simply that she had forgotten her books, or did she need some help? She admitted that she was struggling and could use the help. Monica didn't miss a beat at this point. She suggested that she be allowed to make up for letting Roberta copy her paper by tutoring her because she felt quite confident that she understood the assignment. By this time we were all very involved, with the girls chattering away and figuring it all out.

I realized we were about out of time. This part of the meeting took about thirty minutes. I began writing the agreement (Step 5) on the Student/Teacher Agreement form (see page 118, Part 5). We wondered about what we should tell the rest of the class since the girls knew most of them were aware of what was going on. They decided they wanted to let everyone know how the problem had been solved. They would both tell the class what the agreement was when we gathered after lunch. We decided to have our Follow-Up Meeting (Step 6) as soon as Roberta turned in the assignment and I corrected it. We set that time for lunch the next day.

Monica and Roberta never cheated again. I believe their willingness to be open with the rest of the class and the restoring aspects of the agreement helped many others to not cheat as well.

Roxanne's Experience

Roxanne: When I get to the end of a student/teacher meeting that goes as well as this one did, I am energized rather than drained as the day continues. What an incredible experience of transformation. I knew that the girls were going to be cooperative. Both of these students would be much better prepared for the standardized test when it came along. Both were now aware of how their actions had an effect on others. All of us formed closer, deeper bonds through the process and the completion of the agreement, which restored the trust we all had in each other. Our classroom community became a better place as a result, rather than one in which Roberta and Monica felt uncomfortable. In fact, they felt so good about the agreement that they voluntarily wanted their parents to know what had happened. I felt energized because rather than feeling off task, as I often have felt when using punishment discipline, I felt that all of the time was spent on task because the whole experience was one of teaching and learning.

I know some of you are thinking you would never have time to do any of this. I think it is time incredibly well spent because problems are so well resolved that they do not happen over and over again. The time I spent having lunch and working with these two wonderful people was an hour and a half total (we took another lunch period to go over Roberta's completed homework and to celebrate the completion of that portion of the agreement). The time energized me to be with the rest of my students because it was a time of relationship building.

We <u>did not enter a power struggle cycle</u>. Roberta, being a leader, would not have been afraid of such a struggle because she has been in them before. Such a struggle would look like this: At the moment of being discovered cheating, she would have had to allow me to be in the circle with power over her because I am the teacher and cheating is against the rules. However, she might still have been angry that I discovered her in a situation where she had to admit it and could not lie. This does not have to be anger based on logic. Because getting a detention might be experienced by her as losing face, she would look for an opportunity to get power back. This might be going home to tell her parents that it was not fair (she might say she knows of lots of people who cheat and nothing happens to them), and she had been embarrassed in front of everyone. You can see that a lot of time would be needed to figure this all out. It might never be figured out. I might eventually feel either like I was walking on eggshells, or like I needed to get her out of my class. In either case she could have easily become the student I might have said I was glad to have absent now and then, because the day would be more relaxed and go more smoothly. What happened instead was the opposite of that. Both DTR and punitive discipline take time and energy. DTR leads to more cooperation and understanding. Punitive discipline would have left our community less sure of one another, creating stress and tension for all of us. Time spent in making and keeping agreements builds trust in the community, whereas punitive measures diminish trust.

It is important for me to include the reminder that none of this happens by chance. I follow a structure called *A Peacemaking Process*. It is based on the Peacemaking Model developed by Ron (see Part 2) that carries me along in my decisions as the leader in a step-by-step process that continues to constructively escalate the conflict and invite cooperation until the conflict gets resolved. The DTR Flowchart and the Peacemaking Process are proven processes that work. That does not mean there is not effort involved in carrying them out. It takes commitment and work to put these structures into practice and then to sustain them. I think the effort it takes is worth it because it builds community and promotes learning at each step.

What follows is a description of *A Peacemaking Model* (Part 2) and then the specific step-by-step strategy we call a Peacemaking Process (Part 3).

Part 2

A Peacemaking Model

The Theoretical Model that Guides the Student/Teacher Meeting

This model provides direction for the student/teacher meeting Roxanne described. Ron developed the model while observing meetings between crime victims and offenders who had an injustice between them and then moved to a place where it was no longer a barrier to a civil relationship. In some cases they moved to a caring relationship. The pattern was condensed into what Ron calls *A Peacemaking Model*. This model provides the theory behind a Peacemaking Process that Roxanne uses to guide her in a Student/Teacher Meeting or Family Conference.

Ron will briefly describe both how the model emerged and how he understands the elements of the model. (For additional information on the Peacemaking Model see articles: *A Peacemaking Model* and *A Peacemaking Model: A Biblical Perspective* at peace.fresno. edu/docs/model.shtml

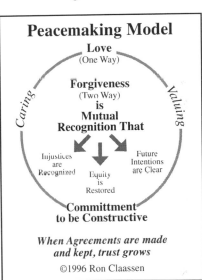

Developing A Peacemaking Model

Ron: In 1982, I helped found a Victim Offender Reconciliation Program (VORP) in Fresno, California. I was the director of VORP until November 1999, and, while no longer as involved in the day-to-day details, I continue active participation. The Center for Peacemaking provides the ongoing administrative oversight of VORP, and I am the director of the Center. Fresno VORP trains volunteers from the community, who meet first with the offender and then with the victim. If both are willing to meet to search for a constructive way of dealing with the offense, the mediator helps arrange and then facilitates a meeting. Approximately 37,200 people have participated in a VORP peacemaking process in Fresno County.

The following stories are just two of thousands from Fresno since VORP was established in 1982 (read more VORP stories at vorp.org/vorpnews—scroll down to 1999 for Ron's stories).

One teenage girl stole another's purse. There wasn't much money in the purse, but the sense of violation was intense and the animosity it created between them was seriously escalating. VORP was asked to work with them. In separate meetings with each of the girls, the mediator listened to their experiences and then invited them to consider "making things as right as possible." They each agreed. Surrounded by friends and parents, they each told how they experienced the event, the other summarized, they discussed what they could do to make things as right as possible between them (apology, returning the purse, and paying back the money) and they developed a plan to improve their future relationship. Agreements were written and signed, and a follow-up meeting was scheduled. They kept their agreements, and they, along with their families and friends, were relieved and happy with the outcome.

Two boys were upset with their school for ending a sports program that was very important to them. They went to their principal's home with a pipe bomb. The principal heard something, went out to investigate, and had just gone back into the house when the bomb exploded. The force of the bomb broke two windows and sent a rose bush onto their neighbor's roof. The principal might have been killed or seriously injured if he had been outside. The boys were identified and admitted what they had done. VORP was contacted, and, after separate meetings, led a series of meetings with as many as twenty people. The boys acknowledged what they had done and listened intently to the principal and his wife describe their experience and intense feelings at the time of the bombing and up to the point of the meeting. The whole group discussed what could be done to repair the damage and demonstrate the boy's commitment to a constructive future. They also discussed the reasons for the cancellation of the sports program and made some mutually acceptable agreements. Agreements were written and follow-up meetings were scheduled. Over the years, and as the agreements were kept, a high degree of satisfaction with the process and outcome was reported.

While I observed many cases with similar positive results, not all cases were as positive. A concern I had was that simply encouraging an encounter or even arranging an encounter does not necessarily mean it will be a constructive encounter.

In my years of working with VORP, I looked for what it was that increased the likelihood that an encounter would be constructive. Perhaps because I was a mathematics teacher in my first career, I began searching for patterns among those cases that ended with a high degree of reconciliation.

While VORP represented a particular type of conflict, it seemed to me that another way to search for the same pattern would be to ask people two questions and listen to their stories. "Have you ever had an experience where something happened to make your relationship with someone bad, and then later that relationship was good? Would you be willing to tell me what happened to make that possible?" I have listened to many wonderful stories. As I listened, a pattern emerged. The story that best illustrates the pattern is from Johnny (his real name).

Johnny was part of an informal summer peacemaking camp at a local park. All of the kids at this camp had lost a sibling or in some way been deeply injured by gang violence. Nancy, the dedicated and creative leader of the camp, invited me to join them one morning. She gave me permission to ask the campers those two questions. Johnny, eleven years old, raised his hand enthusiastically.

This is his story:

> My brother was gone for the weekend to San Francisco. My friends and I went into his room. We were not supposed to. We just had fun at first but then we trashed it and broke his boom box. When he got home, he was really mad. But he didn't hit me. He wanted to know if I did it. I told him my friends and I did it. He wanted to know if my friends and I would clean it up. I told him we would. He wanted to know if we would fix the boom box. I told him we would. He wanted to know if the next time he was gone, if we would stay out of his room. We told him we would. We cleaned his room, fixed the boom box, and have stayed out of his room, and everything is cool.

In the time remaining that morning, Johnny and I worked together (as mediators) to see if we could use his brother's pattern to help the others solve problems they made up and role-played.

I really like Johnny's story because it is so simple yet so clearly illustrates a pattern. This pattern is very similar to the VORP stories I observed and to other reconciliation stories I have heard from many people who have answered the same two questions.

Identifying a Pattern

The pattern Johnny's story illustrates has five parts.

Part 1—*A Commitment to be Constructive*

Johnny's brother decided to be constructive with Johnny even though Johnny's actions had been destructive toward him. Peacemaking starts when the one offended does not respond in kind.

Part 2—*Recognizing the Injustice*

Johnny's brother asked if Johnny had messed up his room, and Johnny acknowledged that he and his friends had done it. This second part of the process or pattern, recognizing the injustice, is when all of the parties describe their experience and feelings and have them recognized by the other(s).

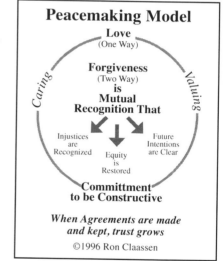

This part of the pattern can happen in many different ways, and the time required for this part varies greatly. In some cases, it happens quickly and in others it may take a long time. In some cases, it happens directly and in some cases it happens in less direct ways or even in intentionally indirect ways.

Part 3—*Restoring Equity*

In Johnny's story, once the injustice was recognized, the next part was to repair the damage as much as possible. Johnny and his brother decided it would help if Johnny and his friends would clean up the room and fix the broken boom box.

This third part I refer to as Restoring Equity. In stories where relationships move from bad to good, something is done to repair the damage and to restore equity as much as possible.

Part 4—*Clarifying Future Intentions*

In Johnny's story, the fourth part of the process was to make an agreement about not going into his brother's room and messing it up again.

Agreements to clarify future intentions are designed to prevent a repeat of the offense or injustice and to create a constructive future for all of the parties. Johnny's brother wanted to know if Johnny had changed. He wanted to know if he would do it again, and Johnny assured him of his constructive intentions.

Part 5—*Follow-up and Accountability*

Johnny ended his story with, "And we did all of the things we agreed to do and now everything is cool." Johnny did not end his story with the agreements that were made. He knew intuitively that, for them to get to the place where things were good again between him and his brother, keeping the agreements that had been made was essential.

The fifth part of the pattern is follow-up and accountability. In stories where things that were once bad are now good, agreements that have been made have been kept and have been acknowledged as having been kept.

I have observed that stories that leave out the follow-up part don't experience as much movement from things being bad toward things being good. This seems to be true in both serious and minor offenses.

Parts 2, 3, and 4 (recognizing the injustice, restoring equity, and clarifying the future) are the core elements in what I have often referred to as a three-part process. But I am convinced that they are most helpful when Parts 1 (preparation) and 5 (follow-up) surround them, as illustrated in Johnny's story.

One of the problems of writing this peacemaking pattern as a five-part process is that one might assume it is a linear pattern or process. The order I have used is the order identified by Johnny's story. While most stories I have listened to include these five parts, the order of the parts varies from story to story. The model (see figure) makes the elements look a little less linear.

The Visual—*A Peacemaking Model*

The outside circle of the Peacemaking Model has the words, *Love* (agape), *Valuing, Caring,* and *Commitment to be Constructive. One Way* (under the word *Love*) indicates that each person can make the decision to adopt these qualities independently. This decision by at least one of the persons is needed to get the process started. Inside the circle it says that *Forgiveness is the mutual recognition* that *injustices are recognized,* that *equity is restored* and that the *future intentions are clear.* I am suggesting that forgiveness is discovered when there is a *mutual recognition (Two Way)* that these

three parts are completed. Below the circle you will see "*When Agreements are Made and Kept, Trust Grows.*" This is the follow-up and accountability part of the process.

The student/teacher meeting and the family conference are guided by this Peacemaking Model. The specifics for doing each part of the model are shaped by culture and personality. Following is one specific way to implement the model. We call it, "A Peacemaking Process," the strategy that we use in the student/teacher meeting.

Part 3

A Peacemaking Process

One Step-by-Step Strategy for Leading a Student/Teacher Meeting

When the Four Options Model stop on the Flowchart results in a decision to use #4 or #3 to respond to a conflict, violation or misbehavior, the next question is, "How are we going to do this?" Sometimes just talking and listening to each other is enough. But often teachers abandon #3 or #4 and resort to #1 or #2 because their strategy (or lack of a conscious strategy) was unsuccessful in finding a cooperative agreement and therefore they missed an opportunity to build trust. DTR has at its core the value of building trust by making and keeping cooperative agreements. As Roxanne has described, her success in making agreements with students is not left to chance. She has some very specific step-by-step strategies that she utilizes.

The strategy she follows is called A Peacemaking Process. As you will see, it is a step-by-step implementation of the Peacemaking Model. Following is a brief description of the steps and some rationale for each step.

The step-by-step strategy is written as if there are two parties. It is written so it can be utilized in both #3 and #4 (since a #3 is a facilitated #4). The process can be modified to accommodate more than two parties, as will be illustrated when we move to the Family Conference stop on the Flowchart (Chapter 10). The **bold print** provides the basic instructions for each step. The comments that follow the bold print provide additional instructions for implementation and an abbreviated commentary explaining the rationale of each step. An extended version with additional detail and complexity is beyond the scope of this book. The shortest version can be found on what we call the Yellow Card (see both sides below, available at disciplinethatrestores.org).

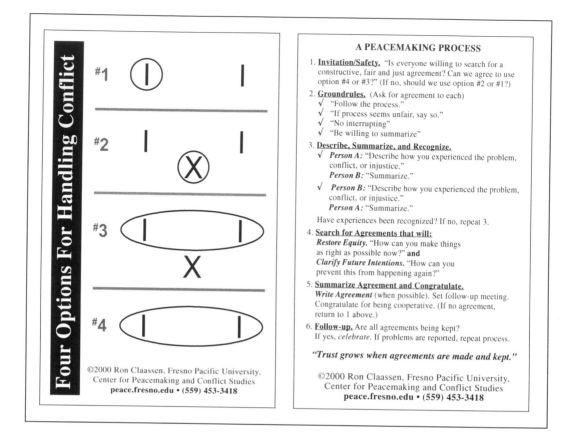

Four Options For Handling Conflict

©2000 Ron Claassen. Fresno Pacific University.
Center for Peacemaking and Conflict Studies
peace.fresno.edu • (559) 453-3418

A PEACEMAKING PROCESS

1. **Invitation/Safety.** "Is everyone willing to search for a constructive, fair and just agreement? Can we agree to use option #4 or #3?" (If no, should we use option #2 or #1?)

2. **Groundrules.** (Ask for agreement to each)
   √ "Follow the process."
   √ "If process seems unfair, say so."
   √ "No interrupting"
   √ "Be willing to summarize"

3. **Describe, Summarize, and Recognize.**
   √ *Person A:* "Describe how you experienced the problem, conflict, or injustice."
   Person B: "Summarize."
   √ *Person B:* "Describe how you experienced the problem, conflict, or injustice."
   Person A: "Summarize."
   Have experiences been recognized? If no, repeat 3.

4. **Search for Agreements that will:**
   Restore Equity. "How can you make things as right as possible now?" **and**
   Clarify Future Intentions. "How can you prevent this from happening again?"

5. **Summarize Agreement and Congratulate.**
   Write Agreement (when possible). Set follow-up meeting. Congratulate for being cooperative. (If no agreement, return to 1 above.)

6. **Follow-up.** Are all agreements being kept? If yes, *celebrate*. If problems are reported, repeat process.

"Trust grows when agreements are made and kept."

©2000 Ron Claassen. Fresno Pacific University.
Center for Peacemaking and Conflict Studies
peace.fresno.edu • (559) 453-3418

We suggest having a copy of the process in front of you when you lead either a #3 or #4 (following a proven process provides safety and confidence). We would also suggest having copies for all parties to follow. When first using the strategy, you might want to use the slightly extended version below.

Start by letting the parties know that you will be following the process they have in front of them. Read the bold print for the first part of Step One and then do what it instructs you to do. When you complete that, read the next step, do it, and continue until you work your way through all parts of all of the steps. The time it takes depends primarily on the complexity and intensity of the conflict (fifteen to thirty minutes in most school cases). The first several times you use this strategy, it is very important to complete all of the parts of all of the steps. If being that thorough feels uncomfortable, tell the people who are participating that you have been instructed to do all of the steps, and at the end you would like their evaluation to help you decide if some of the steps could or should have been left out. Tell them that you need their help to complete this assignment. If you don't do all of the parts of all of the steps, you will never understand the value of each. After several times through, reread this chapter to compare your experience with the rationale provided. We wish you the best as you utilize this amazing process.

Step 1: Preparation, Invitation/Safety

We are assuming that the teacher will be the leader of the process in a #4 student/teacher meeting. (If doing this as a #3, the mediator will lead the process.) Preparation is very important. If teachers and students agree to be constructive and search for agreements, the process will be successful. If they don't agree to these, it is likely one or the other will find ways to block agreements. Agreed upon structure provides safety and increases hope for a fair process. Some tension and awkwardness is normal in the early stages of the process. The Introduction and ground rules take no more than two to five minutes to cover in most cases.

A. **Introductions (if needed).** In most student/teacher meetings, this step is not needed. But if the student is a new student or you are a substitute teacher, one-minute introductions may be helpful and/or needed.

B. **Briefly state conflict that needs to be resolved.** This should be a short sentence or two at the most. It should be stated in a way that both the student and teacher can agree to it. "We have been having problems when I start a lesson," or "We seem to have some confusion about how we are going to implement the respect agreement." This is not the place to say, "You have been disruptive when…" This is not the time for a full discussion of the situation. That will come later.

C. **Look at, describe, and discuss the Four Options Model, and decide or confirm if all parties want to use #4 (or #3).** Even if a misbehaving student agreed to #4 at the time of the offense, this is still an important step. The purpose of doing this is to eliminate confusion regarding who will make the decision and to increase commitment to seeking mutual understanding and agreement. Emphasize that while many ideas and possibilities may be discussed, there is no "agreement" until everyone inside the circle (teacher and student) agrees. The teacher might say the following while pointing to each as described, "In #1,

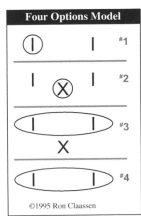

one person has all of the power and the other is expected to go along, like a police officer making an arrest. In #2, an outside authority makes the decision, like a principal making a decision for two students in conflict. In #3 and #4, there is no decision until the parties agree. I am willing to do a #4, are you?"

D. **Describe and discuss the Issues/Commitment to be Constructive Model and decide or confirm if all parties agree to work in the upper right quadrant.**

The model illustrates that it is possible to have strong and even mutually exclusive positions on issues and still be committed to being constructive in the process of seeking agreements that address the issues. The teacher might say, "Can we both agree to address the issues and be constructive? I can, can you?" (It is helpful to point to the upper right-hand quadrant while asking this question.) If a student or teacher cannot agree to do both, they are not ready. Ask "Why not?" and use your Active Listening and I-Message skills (Chapter 5). Or, make a referral to the Thinkery (Chapter 9).

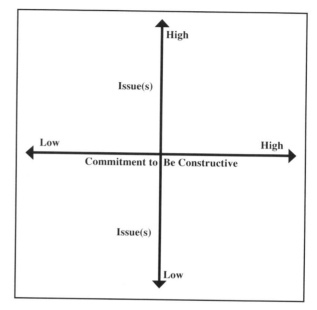

Step 2: Ground Rules

The invitation/preparation stage and now the ground rules are not intended to stifle discussion, disagreement or expression of strong feelings, but to create a safe and respectful environment in which problems, disagreements, violations, injustices, etc. can be openly expressed, discussed and transformed into new understandings and constructive agreements. It is important that both teacher and student agree to follow each ground rule. The teacher might say, "In order to have a fair and constructive process, it is helpful if we each agree to the following ground rules." (Read the four bold print ground rules below.) "I can agree. Do they seem like good and constructive ground rules? Can you also agree to each of them?"

- **Follow the process. Allow teacher (or mediator) to lead the process.**
- **If process is not fair, say so.**

While these two ground rules are important on their own, it is important to recognize that they are connected to each other, since both address the issue of power. The two need to be addressed together to achieve a fair power arrangement. The first is an acknowledgement that someone is needed to lead the process, and the second is inviting everyone to be judges of fairness to prevent the leader from having an unfair power advantage. The second provides the student (all parties) a way to also take the lead by raising the fairness issue. If there is a problem with fairness during the process, it takes priority, needs to be stated, and adjustments need to be made to reestablish fairness.

- **Listen without interrupting**
- **Be willing to summarize**

The purpose of these two ground rules is to ensure that all people will be able to express their thoughts and know that they have been listened to and understood. The first ensures that the speaker is able to tell about his or her experience without interruption. (An exception to this would be if one wanted to raise the fairness issue.) The second ensures that the speaker is heard.

A summary is not a statement of agreement. Rather, it is an attempt by the listener to convey to the speaker that the listener has heard and understood what the other was saying and as the speaker intended it to be heard (for more information on Active Listening and I-Messages, see Chapter 5).

Step 3: Describe, Summarize, Recognize the Problem/Hurt/Violation/Injustice

Recognition (giving voice to each person) is the focus of this part of the process. Although additional recognition will happen throughout the process, when hurts or violations are part of the conflict, it is unlikely that repair can be done or that the future can be discussed meaningfully until each person's experience is recognized *by the person(s) that the speaker wants to be sure has heard.* The steps below are written as if there are just two parties. If there are more than two parties, ask the speaker whom she or he would like to do the summarizing. The speaker needs to have the opportunity to choose who will listen and summarize. This is very important because the criteria for moving on to the next step is for the parties to agree that their experiences of the conflict or violation have been recognized.

Decide who will be Person A and Person B.

If one is more powerful (such as the teacher who is leading the meeting), offer some options to the other. A teacher might say to the student, "Do you want to start? Do you want me to start? Or do you want to flip a coin to decide who starts?"

A. Person A describes how he or she experienced the problem/hurt/violation/ injustice (both thoughts and feelings).

If the student chooses to speak first, the teacher might say, "Please describe how you experienced our conflict/problem. When you are finished I will summarize what you said." The language (describe your experience) for the instruction has been chosen very deliberately since what is most helpful at this point in the process is a clear I-message, one that states the experience of the speaker. If the instruction to the speaker is, "So what is the problem?" the speaker will most likely make a You-message, "The problem is that you…" If it is not possible to provide training for each party on how to construct an I-message, inviting the speaker to "describe your experience" will usually elicit one.

Some will start with thoughts and others with feelings. The process encourages all parties (teachers and students) to describe both thoughts and feelings. If a student is having a difficult time starting, the teacher might add, "Describe what happened, along with where, when and how you felt when this was happening." A "feelings chart" might be helpful.

B. Person B restates/summarizes until Person A says, "Yes, that is what I said."

The listener has been told before the speaker started that she would be summarizing. When the experience is of significant length, the speaker may prefer to stop occasionally for a summary, or the speaker may prefer to have the listener take notes so that the speaker can speak without interruption. The instruction to the listener is, "Summarize, using your own words as much as possible, what the speaker said. Be careful to just summarize the speaker's thoughts and feelings. Do not add your own thoughts or feelings at this point." It may be helpful to remind the listener that summarizing does not mean agreement, just that one has heard and understood. This time belongs to the speaker and is not completed until the speaker says, "Yes, that is what I said."

C. Person B describes how she or he experienced the problem/hurt/violation/ injustice (both thoughts and feelings).

This is to give the listener a chance to be the speaker. The process is the same as above. The focus throughout this step should be on the speaker's experiences, thoughts and feelings. If there are more than two parties or "sides," then each should be given a turn and each should designate someone to do the summarizing.

D. Person A restates until Person B says, "Yes, that is what I said."

Throughout the restating/summarizing process, the speaker is invited to make corrections, clarifications and additions as needed to be sure that her or his perspective is heard and understood.

It is time to move on to Step 4 when each person agrees that he or she has been heard. When everyone has been given a chance to speak and be heard, the teacher might say, "I feel like you heard and understood my experience, and I am wondering if you think that I have heard and understood your experience?" If something has not been heard, ask the speaker to repeat it, then ask the listener to summarize, and then ask the same question again. There may or may not be agreement on what happened. If there is not agreement at this point, don't worry—this is not unusual, and it is not a deterrent to moving forward with the process. What is important is that each has been able to express his or her perspective and be heard. It is very unlikely that more speaking and listening will cause one to change her/his perspective.

Step 3 is often the most emotional time in the process. When it is completed, the parties often feel much better because they have been heard but they may feel worse that the other still has a different perspective. In either case, it is time to move forward in the process. It is important to not stop here. Remember, trust grows when agreements are made and kept. The preparation and speaking/listening has created an opportunity to make agreements.

Step 4 is designed to help the parties search for agreements that will repair the recognized problems/hurts/violations/injustices as much as possible, prevent them from happening again, and create a better future. But if the parties have not agreed on what happened, they might be thinking, "If we can't even agree on what happened, how can we possibly trust each other enough to make agreements about Restoring Equity and Future Intentions?" It is not necessary or expected at this point that trust should be or has to be high. If trust were high, the parties would not need this process. If agreements are made and kept, trust will grow.

Step 4: Search for Agreements that Will Restore Equity and Clarify Future Intentions

A teacher might say, "Now that we have listened to each other's experiences, we need to do two things: [1]restore equity (deciding on specifics that will make things as right as possible between us) and [2]clarify future intentions (deciding on specifics that will prevent the problem from happening again and create a good future for both of us). One way to work at this is for each of us to write our ideas privately. Then on a large sheet (divide a paper in half; label the left side *Restore Equity* and the right side *Clarify Future*—see figure) we will record all of our ideas. Then, we will decide on which items we agree. When the agreement looks good to each of us, we will sign it. So let's start by each of us thinking about what specific things will help us restore equity and clarify our future intentions."

Restore Equity	Clarify Future

After a time of private writing (the reason for this is to balance power so this can all be done verbally in minor conflicts and/or with young students), the leader writes one idea from one and one from the other until all are recorded on the large sheet. After they are all recorded, the teacher might say, "Now, let's put a check mark by those on which we both agree. After we have this list, we will record our agreement on the Teacher/Student Agreement Form." Once it is recorded, read the agreement back and then say, "Does this sound like our agreement? Are there any changes you would suggest? Are we ready to sign?" This moment, right after completing the signing, is a good time for a minor celebration and a reminder of the follow-up meeting. Note together that trust grows when agreements are made and kept.

A. Restore Equity

In some teacher/student conflict situations, one is the offender, the other the victim, and everyone agrees. In these cases restoring equity is a one-way process. However, in most conflicts, each feels like the victim and sees the other as the offender. So in these cases, each will need to consider how to restore equity.

"Restoring Equity" is a term that will most likely need some explanation in a student/teacher meeting. It is what makes things as right as possible between parties now. Often it includes apology, but not always. It is a combination of specific things that can be done (like paying for damages, often referred to as *restitution*) and letting go of what is left (often referred to as *grace* but also referred to as *forgiveness* by some.) The grace portion is at the total discretion of the victim both on whether to let go and when to let go. This part is not negotiated. So restore equity, for the purposes of this process, refers to the tangible part of the repair that can be done and includes the grace portion if the victim requests that it be included. Many victims report that when the offender recognizes the injustice, restores equity as much as possible, clarifies constructive future intentions, and then keeps these agreements, the grace part happens quite naturally.

The grace portion is totally at the discretion of the victim. I prefer to reserve the word *forgiveness* for the discovery that is made when the entire process is completed— injustices are recognized and the agreements to restore equity and clarify the future are made, kept, and acknowledged as having been kept. The mutual recognition of the transformation that is experienced or discovered is forgiveness. Teachers who have been happy when a particular student was absent (because she or he made the teacher's life so difficult) and students who dreaded coming to class (because the teacher made their lives so difficult) have reported feeling pleased to be together in class after completing this entire process. That discovery is real forgiveness as I understand it.

B. Clarify Future Intentions

Agreements that clarify future intentions address what will create a better future for each individual as well as clarifying the future relationship of the parties. The agreement generally includes a statement regarding intentions related to non-repetition of the offense(s), specific behaviors or actions that will make life better for each of them and their relationship, as well as what accountability might be helpful to encourage and support each party in keeping the agreement(s). It should include expectations regarding how they will relate to each other in the future. If they rarely see each other, what are their expectations if they do meet? If they see each other frequently, the first agreement might clarify expectations between the time of the agreement and the first follow-up meeting. At the follow-up meeting, the expectations might be discussed again and perhaps modified until the next follow-up meeting. If agreements are made and kept, trust will grow, and the time will come when the relationship is like any good relationship.

Step 5. Evaluate, Write, Summarize, and Celebrate the Agreement

A. Evaluate the chosen options: are they reasonable, respectful, and restorative for all parties? Modify the agreement if necessary.

This step provides additional criteria for evaluating which options are appropriate. Some people might be willing to accept agreements that do not meet these higher standards. The importance of these criteria becomes clearer when placing each on a continuum. If an agreement is on the opposite side of the continuum, i.e., unreasonable, disrespectful, and intended to stigmatize or ostracize, most people would consider that abusive. A teacher might say, "Now that we have agreed on some specific items that we think will restore equity and clarify our future constructive intentions, another evaluation criteria is to ask ourselves: 'Is our agreement reasonable, respectful, restorative, and reintegrative for both of us?'" Roxanne says that children both understand and value these additional criteria.

B. Craft/write the final agreement

When in doubt about whether or not to write the agreement, write it. The purpose of writing the agreement is to reduce the likelihood that each will have a different memory of the agreement. If the agreement is not written and each has a different memory of what has been agreed, it is very likely that each will think the other is not keeping the agreement. When this happens, trust is diminished because each thinks the other is not keeping the agreement.

The purpose of writing is to clarify and memorialize the agreement, not an attempt to force people to keep it. People will keep an agreement that they helped construct and that they think is reasonable, respectful, restorative, and reintegrative. Many do report that the symbolic act of signing an agreement does add to their commitment.

C. Sign and Celebrate. Congratulate each other for hard work and cooperative spirit.

When the agreement is written but before it is signed, it is important that the leader ask the question for everyone to consider: "Where could this agreement be misunderstood or in some way fail?" If concerns are raised, they should be discussed and the agreement should be modified accordingly. It is important to thank the person who raised the concerns since this is the best time to address and remedy potential problems.

Finally, it is important to decide on a date and time for a follow-up meeting. At least one follow-up meeting should be scheduled. Roxanne finds that when working with a student who is trying to modify a long-term habit, several follow-up meetings may be required. When identifying a date for the meeting, think of both the time needed to carry out the agreements and the difficulty of keeping the agreements. It is better to have a meeting too soon rather than too late. If the parties disagree about how long to wait, we suggest using the shortest date for the first meeting. Students usually welcome and look forward to a follow-up meeting, whereas adults often resist them or see them as unnecessary (until they experience their value). That is why we introduce the follow-up meeting as part of the process, not an optional add-on.

Step 6: Follow-up Meeting(s)

Follow-up is an essential part of the Peacemaking Process. Since it is so important and happens later, not at the meeting, it is a separate stop on the Flowchart (see Chapter 8). A follow-up meeting provides the occasion for acknowledging whether agreements have been kept. I sometimes say that one-third of the work of the Peacemaking Process is preparation, one-third is the listening, summarizing, and agreement making, and one-third is the follow-up. Having a follow-up meeting increases the likelihood of long-term value emerging from the efforts. If you meet and all agreements are being kept, celebration is in order and trust will grow. If part or all of the agreement is not being kept, the follow-up meeting provides a forum to address the problem.

Part 4

Peacemaking Process Stories

The Peacemaking Process that we have just examined is designed to assist people who have experienced a conflict and who are open to searching for a way to make things as right as possible between the parties. Roxanne notes that most conflicts in schools soon escalate to involve some violation or hurt, and that is why we have emphasized this strategy. She would say that 95% of the time this is the strategy she uses.

It is important to keep in mind that A Peacemaking Process is a strategy designed for people who considered the Four Options Model and decided to work cooperatively (#3 or #4). No strategy will help people find a cooperative resolution if even one of the parties does not desire it. That is why the preliminaries, including each party's commitment to be constructive, are an essential part of the process.

I give this assignment to teachers: "I want you to try out the Peacemaking Process with a student who adds a lot of stress to your life. Pick the student who, if she or he is absent, you know your day will be a lot more pleasant. Use the Four Options Model to invite the student to do #4 with you. If he or she agrees, use the Peacemaking Process to address the conflicts and violations between you. Then write a brief reflection and be prepared to tell us about your experience in class." Below are two stories from teachers who took on this assignment. I have paraphrased their stories. One is a high school story and the other a kindergarten story.

A High School Student/Teacher Meeting Story

"I knew exactly with which student I should try out this process. I have been a high school teacher for over ten years, and I am pretty authoritarian. It works for me, at least with most students. It hadn't worked with Terry. He does something to disturb me and those around him every time I start a lesson. I tried giving him the 'evil eye,' giving him detentions, sending him to the counselors, sending notes to his parents. Instead of getting better, he resisted me even more and made my day more miserable. I really wanted to get him transferred out of my class.

"I was pretty skeptical about using these processes because they seemed somewhat weak to me. I decided that since you gave the assignment, I would use it with Terry to show that this process really wouldn't work. Since he is most disturbing when I start a lesson, I decided to ask my student teacher to take over the class when he started his usual disruptions, and I would take him out of the class and 'try out' this step-by-step peacemaking process.

"We didn't have to wait long until he started his usual disruptive behavior. I asked him to come outside with me, and my student teacher took over with the rest of the class. When we got outside, I showed him the Four Options Model and explained to him that I was supposed to say that I would like to do #4 with him and then ask him if he would be willing to do #4 with me. He understood the model immediately and he didn't hesitate; he said he would also prefer #4. That really made me mad. If he was really that cooperative, why had he been so disruptive all year?

"I controlled myself and explained to him that in order to do #4 we would have to agree to some ground rules: Allow me to lead the process, tell me if anything seems unfair, no interrupting, no profanity or name calling, and be willing to summarize. He agreed.

"I then told him briefly about the process: we would each describe our experiences and then, after summarizing, we would search for ways to restore equity and clarify our future intentions to prevent the problem from happening again and to create a better relationship for both of us. He agreed to follow the process.

"I asked him if he wanted to start, if he wanted me to start, or if he preferred that we flip a coin to decide who would start. He wanted to start. He said, 'The problem is that you talk too fast and I can't keep up. When I do things, it slows things down and I feel I have a better chance.' I know that I do talk rather fast, and he is a second-language learner. I had to control myself from lashing out at him for not telling me this before, but I had agreed to the process so I summarized. When I finished, he said that that was about it.

"It was now my turn to descibe my experience. I reminded him that he would be summarizing me when I finished. I told him, 'When you disturb me and the others around you, I feel really disespected and frustrated. I have prepared a presentation and because of the disturbance, I get sidetracked and don't complete it as I intended. I often discover later that I left out some of the important parts. It is really frustrating for me. I don't like saying this but it is true—my day goes a lot better when you are absent. I wish it weren't like that.' He summarized what I had said and seemed to understand my perspective. I asked him if he thought I had listened to him and he said yes. I told him that I felt he had really listened to me.

"So the next two things to do were to decide how to restore equity and clarify our future intentions. We decided to talk about the future first. We decided that I would talk slower when making presentations but that if I were not talking slow enough, he would give me a signal. I would then slow down some more or I would give a signal back that meant he should get what he could. Then, after the class started working on their assignments, I would meet with him privately to be sure he understood the presentation. We both thought if we did these things, that would solve the problem in the future.

"We then talked about what it would take to restore equity (repair the damage as much as possible). We apologized to each other, he for not telling me and me for not asking him before this. We both apologized for those times we had been disrespectful to eath other. We both agreed that our failure to resolve this earlier had wasted a lot of class time, so we agreed to announce to the class that we had a plan to resolve our problem and we would apologize to them for wasting their time. We did this, and we have used our signals several times. It is working.

"Now, rather than wishing he were absent, I enjoy greeting him as he walks into the class. I was amazed at how difficult (I had wanted to resort several times to my authoritarian comfort zone) yet helpful it was to follow a process. If it hadn't been an assignment, I'm not sure if I would have ever tried out the process. I am sure our follow-up meetings will be celebrations. I am sure I will use the process again. As I reflect on this experience, trust has grown as a result of the agreements we made."

A Kindergarten Student/Teacher Meeting Story

"I have been a kindergarten teacher for over sixteen years. I was very skeptical that a process this complicated could work with such young students. I have a student who has been somewhat difficult to manage all year. He wouldn't focus on anything very long and didn't follow instructions well at all. Instead of getting better, he has been getting worse throughout the year. Recently he started to lie down on the floor and roll around, bumping into chairs, tables, and other students. I had talked with his parents, and we had begun discussing other options, including medication. I decided to try out the Peacemaking Process with him.

"I started by showing him the Four Options model. When I asked him which options he would prefer, he chose #4 without hesitation. I modified the language some and made each step brief but followed all of the steps. He agreed to the ground rules and wanted me to go first, describing our experiences. I told him I would be asking him to summarize what I said and gave him a few examples. He seemed to understand. He was getting wiggly so I hurried on.

"I told him I was worried about him not learning what he needed to when he didn't participate with the others. I was also worried that he or others might get hurt when he would lie down and roll around the floor. He summarized. I asked him to describe his experience and he said he didn't have anything to say. I summarized this and tried to encourage him to say more but he didn't seem to want to say anything more.

"I then asked him to think about what we might do to prevent the rolling around. He said, 'I could stop doing it.' I thanked him for that idea and asked if I could remind him if he forgot. After thinking a bit, he said, 'If you would smile.' So we wrote in our agreement that he would stop, and that if I reminded him, I would smile.

"It was amazing. He did stop rolling, and when he was off track in other things, I would remember to smile when I reminded him. It hasn't resolved everything but I am amazed at how effective it has been. Our first follow-up meeting was very positive, and we have another scheduled. I will certainly use this process a lot more in the future."

Part 5

Student/Teacher Agreement Form and Instructions

Instructions

Since it is very important to write agreements and since teachers are always short of time, the Student/Teacher Agreement Form was created as a time-saver. It was also created specifically with the Peacemaking Process in mind. You will note that all the major steps in the Peacemaking Process, which is recommended for making student/teacher agreements in Chapter 7, are on the form. You are welcome to duplicate this form, or if you prefer, you can download one from the DTR Website: disciplinethatrestores.org/.

The primary purpose of putting an agreement in writing is to serve as a reliable and common memory of the agreement. Without this common memory, it has been our observation that within a short time all parties have different memories regarding the details. With different memories, each feels that the other has not kept the agreement. Instead of building trust, trust diminishes.

Another purpose of writing an agreement is to clarify the verbal agreement. Sometimes the agreement seems clear in its verbal form but when it is written, it seems different to one or all of the parties. Writing the agreement provides time for each party to clarify what he or she is willing to do and what each expects of the other.

How to Use the Form

The form provides space for a number of preliminary items: the names of the student and teacher, the date of the agreement, a space to check that they are both seeking a constructive resolution, a space to indicate they have agreed to utilize #4 or #3, and a space to state the conflict to be addressed. The statement of the conflict should be very brief. When the conflict is primarily a problem to solve, it should be stated in neutral language so that both sides would say, "Yes, this is the conflict/problem we need to resolve." The statement might be as brief as *homework; teacher and student not getting along well; different expectations for starting a class;* etc. If the problem is a violation of a rule and therefore usually also experienced as an injustice or violation of the teacher, it might be stated as *theft, profanity, dress code,* etc.

Item I (Recognizing the Problem/Injustice/Violation) provides an opportunity to recognize together that both feel that the problem, violation, or injustice was recognized. That means that each person had a chance to describe his or her experience (both facts and feelings) and the other listened enough to be able to summarize so that the speaker would say, "Yes, you have heard me." The one filling out the form (usually the teacher) would read the statement and ask if this item may be checked. The form provides space for additional comments in this area if needed.

Items II and III provide space to record what has been decided to "make things as right as possible" between the teacher and student *now* and for the *future*.

Item II (Restore Equity) provides space for checking if one or both apologized as part or the whole of the restoring equity part of the agreement. This is utilized more when the conflict is a violation or injustice and less when it is primarily a problem to solve. We have noticed in school that apology is a very common part of restoring equity. The space to check apology should just be left blank if there was no need for apology. The "other" space is provided for describing other ways that equity will be or has been restored. Perhaps the offender paid for an item that had been taken, agreed to help the custodian repair something that was broken, or painted over graffiti. Whatever has been agreed to in order to make things right between them *now* should be described in detail (when, who, where, how, etc.). If it was primarily a problem to be solved and both do not see a need for apology, this can be noted in the "other" space.

Item III (Future Intentions) provides space to describe the part of the agreement they have created to prevent reoccurrence of a similar problem by doing something different in the future. This is generally some constructive action that can be observed, supported, and verified. This is where the agreement for constructive change is documented. A space is provided to indicate that the connection between making and keeping agreements and the development of trust has been discussed. Since this discussion is so important, we provided a space to memorialize this discussion. There is also space to indicate if the agreement included asking for some assistance from someone not at the meeting.

Item IV (Follow-up Meeting) provides space to state the details (date, time, location) regarding the follow-up meeting. It is included as part of the agreement because follow-up is very important—almost as important as the agreement itself.

The next space is for the teacher and student signatures. Before signing, it is important to read the entire agreement aloud together so that both are confident that it says what was agreed. The signing is a significant symbolic act adding value to the agreement.

The final space provides a place to record the content of the follow-up meeting. It indicates if the agreements that were made were kept. Most follow-up meetings are a time of acknowledging that the agreements were kept. This formal acknowledgement symbolically brings closure to the conflict. In some cases where trust was very low in the beginning, it might be necessary to have several follow-up meetings before bringing closure. If some agreements were kept and others were not, the space can be used to record how it was decided to deal with the part of the agreement that was not kept. It could refer to a new agreement process and form that adds detail and accountability to areas of the agreement that were not kept the first time.

In all cases, the form should serve as a reminder of the process and a starting point in memorializing the agreement. If an agreement is longer and requires more space for detail, the detail should be written on the back of the form or on another sheet and attached to the form.

Student/Teacher Agreement

Student _____   What is the conflict about? _____

Teacher _____   _____

Date _____   _____

<table>
<tr><td>

We have agreed to search for a constructive resolution.

☐ *YES*   ☐ *NO*

</td><td>

We have agreed to use a cooperative process

☐ *#4*   ☐ *#3*

</td></tr>
</table>

We've met and have discussed the conflict and agreed to the following to make things as right as possible:

I. Recognize Injustice/Violation

☐ We listened to each other's experience (both facts and feelings) and agree that injustices/violations have been recognized.

☐ Other: _____

_____

II. Restore Equity

☐ Apology for injustices/violations.

☐ Other (describe in detail): _____

_____

III. Future Intentions

☐ We agreed to prevent the problem from happening again by: _____

_____

_____

☐ We talked about how important it is to complete this agreement and how this will help build trust.

☐ _____ has asked for help with the following concerns _____

_____

IV. Follow-Up Meeting

We agree to meet again for a follow-up meeting. (date, time, location) _____

_____   _____
Student Signature   Teacher Signature

Follow-up Results: _____

_____

_____

_____

Copyright © 2008 Ron and Roxanne Claassen

Chapter 8 • **Follow-up Meeting(s)**

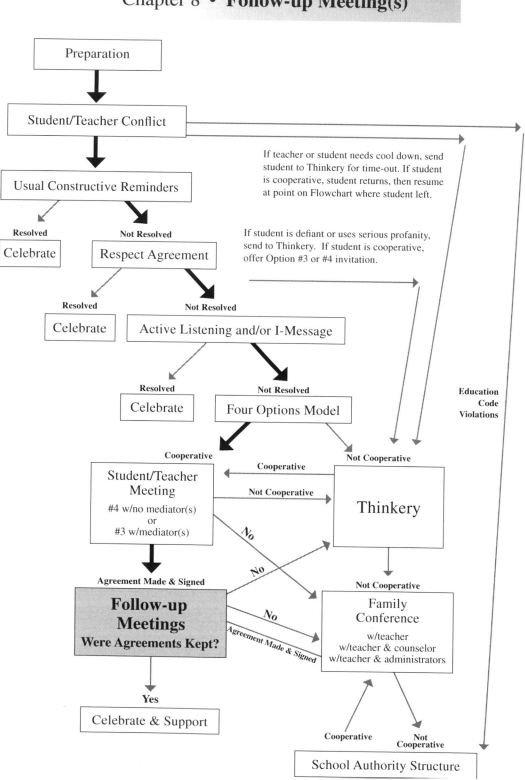

Copyright © 2008 Ron and Roxanne Claassen

Chapter 8
Follow-up Meeting(s)

Introduction

Ron: Trust grows when agreements are made and kept. As noted in Chapter 7, Follow-up Meetings are an essential part of the Peacemaking Process. Since they are so critical in determining the success or failure of a student/teacher agreement, they have been given a separate stop on the DTR Flowchart.

Follow-up meetings (one or more) provide the opportunity for accountability and celebration, both of which are diminished if the teacher leaves out this crucial step. Often by the time you have arrived here (if the agreement is being kept), you think all is going so well that this is not a necessary meeting to have. In reality, things might be going so well in part because of the increased accountability due to planning the follow-up meeting. It is during the follow-up meeting that all who have been involved in the making of the agreement get a chance to look at the agreement formally once again and to recognize together that changes have occurred because the agreement is being kept. This can be a celebration of that accomplishment.

On the other hand, if the agreement or parts of it are not being kept, this is a formal time to recognize this and to work together to either recommit to the agreement as it is written or to modify the agreement so it will be kept. It is a time to figure out what sort of help or changes might be needed in order for you and your student to keep the agreement. It might be that another time of listening and/or I-messages is needed. It is definitely a time of further relationship building. If not all agreements have been kept, another follow-up meeting should be scheduled.

A Follow-up Meeting Process

At a follow-up meeting, the teacher might say, "This is our opportunity to read our agreement and then decide if all of our agreements are being kept. If they are, we need to decide if another follow-up meeting would be helpful. If some or all of the agreements are not being kept, we will need to discuss why and then decide if we should try again. Then, finally, when we are all confident that our agreements are being kept, we need to decide how to celebrate. So, now let's read the agreement." The teacher or student then reads the agreement out loud.

1. Read agreement.

It is best that both can see it or for each person to have a copy.

2. Ask, "Are all agreements being kept?"

In student/teacher agreements, since you are together every day, it is tempting to do the follow-up meeting informally and without input from the student. It seems reasonable for the teacher to just say, "I am proud of the way you have been keeping the agreement. Good job." On the surface this seems good, but what is missing is the opportunity for a mutual recognition, including the student noting that the teacher is also keeping the agreement.

Asking if the agreements have been kept is important, because if they have been kept, trust will grow. This is a chance to recognize and build on it. But, if even one of the parties thinks the agreement has not been kept, the agreement will be viewed as unsuccessful. Trust will be diminished. Unless something is done to explore what happened, the effort to resolve the issue cooperatively will be abandoned. And it is possible that all of this happened just because of a misunderstanding that was not discussed and clarified. Or, it might be because the agreement was not reasonable and needs to be renegotiated.

3. If "no" (some or all of the agreements are not being kept), identify what is not being kept and discuss the options.

If some or all of the agreements have not been kept, the follow-up meeting is an opportunity to find out why. In a student/teacher meeting, the goal is to gain the cooperation of the student. If the first attempt at an agreement did not work, it is worth a second attempt. Start by asking the person saying the agreements are not being kept to identify which part of the agreement he or she means and to describe how it was not kept. Ask the other person to summarize until the original person says, "Yes, that is what I said." Ask, "Does the agreement clearly say what should have been done?" along with, "Does the agreement need to be modified?" You could also ask, "Should we treat this as another problem/hurt/violation and/or injustice?"

If correcting the problem is not accomplished with a simple adjustment, review the Four Options Model, the Issues/Commitment to be Constructive Model, and other introductory commitments and ground rules. If there is a verbal commitment to these, continue with the Peacemaking Process and complete all the steps. Include more accountability in the new agreement. One way to ensure there is more accountability is to agree to include more people who are respected persons from each party's life in the next follow-up meeting. Roxanne's experience is that most students keep the agreements that they helped create. It is rare that this kind of escalation is necessary. It is also important not to give up on any student, and especially one who continues to indicate a willingness to cooperate.

4. If "yes" (all agreements are being kept), celebrate as appropriate. Recognize that trust grows when agreements are made and kept.

In most student/teacher follow-up meetings, the celebration is a smile, a handshake, or perhaps a lunch together at school. In one of my victim/offender meetings, the victim suggested that if their complex yearlong agreement was kept, there should be a celebration. He offered to bring pie. The offender offered to bring ice cream. A year later there was a celebration with pie and ice cream.

An Eighth-Grade Follow-up Meeting Story

The Agreement Had Been Kept

Roxanne: In the story of Roberta, Monica, and me (page 89), the follow-up meeting was set for the next day. This gave Roberta time to get help from Monica to understand the algebra assignment better and to practice it on her own by doing the homework assignment she had not done. We met once again at lunch. We started by reading the agreement. The agreement was for Roberta to do the "copied assignment" on her own. Roberta had her assignment finished. Both girls were anxious to see how Roberta had done on the assignment. I corrected her work with both girls looking over my shoulders. They celebrated a little with each answer that was correct. They discussed the mistakes on each answer that was wrong. This gave both students insight into what goes into helping someone understand a process and why practice that includes showing all the work is so helpful. It also was a chance for seeing mistakes as an opportunity for further learning and insight. I don't recall exactly what Roberta got on the assignment, but I remember the positive experience the three of us had during this follow-up time. Roberta and Monica both regained a sense of self-worth as they saw what they could accomplish together.

Another part of the agreement called for them to share our agreement with the rest of the class. As we discussed this part, both expressed feeling nervous, but when they noticed that everyone listened and nodded, indicating they thought we had come to a good agreement, they actually felt good about themselves and that they could be part of the class again without feeling bad or guilty about anything. In fact, Monica had been asked by a couple of people for help on their algebra. She assured me she had helped and not given them the answers.

I had the chance to ask the girls if there were anything further they wanted me to do or if there were some things they felt I could do that would be more helpful during algebra. They made one or two suggestions that included going a little slower when introducing a new concept and giving plenty of time to practice a few problems in class before giving an assignment. They also suggested that there were sometimes too many problems to practice, especially since we were getting into areas that involved many steps, and therefore it took quite a bit of time to solve each one. They thought two or three of these were enough instead of four or five. We decided that we would work together as a class to decide how many practice problems would be best as each homework assignment was made.

We ended our meeting by deciding that no further follow-up was necessary. We decided to celebrate by having lunch together (this meant we would eat in the classroom instead of the cafeteria) after the next algebra test no matter what the outcome of that test and that we would invite anyone from class who wanted to join us.

In this situation, if we had not had a formal follow-up meeting, many good things would not have happened. There would not have been a time for Roberta and Monica to really be restored to a position of balance in the class and with me. Had I said, "Just give me your homework, and I will correct it and give it back to you later," the girls might have wondered why we had bothered to write the agreement and, worse, they would have thought that I was not a person who kept my agreements. It cannot be said too many times that making and keeping agreements is what leads to trust. Our trust in each other was greatly built through this experience.

A Sixth-Grade Follow-up Meeting Story

The Agreement Had Not Been Kept

Roxanne: When an agreement is not being kept, follow-up becomes a crucial step in helping a student or students reevaluate their actions and their commitment to cooperate. As quickly as possible, figure out with a student what is preventing him or her from keeping the agreement so you can create a plan together that will help the student succeed. These are often situations in which a long-standing habit of a particular behavior needs to change. As we all know, a habit is difficult to change. If follow-up is not practiced, the student does not experience the support and accountability needed for change. In fact, lack of follow-up may be part of the pattern they have had with adults that actually reinforces the old habit.

Many of us have a difficult student in class who unfortunately causes us to breathe a sigh of relief when she or he is absent. This student often has a set of long-standing behaviors that have somehow been reinforced over the years rather than diminished. A student who reaches the eighth grade with these kinds of disruptive habits can be quite challenging. I have found that it is possible to effect change if I am diligent in making agreements with such students and willing to do the follow-up work required until they begin to self-monitor and are successful in keeping the agreements they have made.

One such student for me, Steve, loved to begin a "comedy" act in my science class as new and difficult material was being introduced. This was a silent act meant for his particular friends. It was very distracting not only for the friends but for me and the other students as well. We went through all the steps on the Flowchart rather quickly and had a teacher/student meeting (Option #4) that resulted in a good agreement, giving us time to discuss the importance of listening and not distracting others, especially when material was new. Steve acknowledged that he did this and that he did this more during subjects that came less easily to him (described by him as "boring," which gave us a chance to discuss who was really in charge of whether or not we were bored) than during subjects that were of high interest and came more easily to him. Science, if it were not about snakes, just did not grab his interest. He apologized, but was not sure he could stop. Our agreement for the future was that when he started the behavior, I would signal him by walking over close to him and putting my hand on his desk and standing there until he nodded that he knew what I was telling him. This worked very well the first few times. But after a day or two, he began ignoring the signal.

Usually follow-up is scheduled after the agreement has been in place for at least a week. It became clear that Steve and I needed to meet sooner if we wanted to see some change. As Steve ignored my signal, I got the class to a point where students could turn to a neighbor to talk about what they were hearing. I used this time to talk to Steve. Using an I-message, I told him what I was experiencing and asked him if we could meet at break. He agreed. At break, I took out our agreement, and we read it out loud. I said that I wondered if the agreement was being kept. He said he knew he wasn't keeping it. It felt odd to stop what he was in the habit of doing, and he was being egged on by the friends who were missing the distraction. We discussed whether or not we needed to change some things in the agreement. I wondered if there were more or other things I could do that would be more helpful. We wondered if we needed to invite the friends to help us, or Steve's parents to help us. In the end, Steve decided the agreement was fine, he just needed to stop. He still needed the signal a few times, but this became less and less. As is usually the case, with support and accountability, he eventually did stop. He just needed a little more escalation of the cooperative process to decide it was up to him. Steve earned the best grade he had ever received in science that year. That was a great celebration to him since he got $5 for each A he brought home. He also gradually began to find science less boring since he was engaging with it rather than avoiding it.

A Fourth-Grade Follow-up Story after an Option #3

Roxanne: This situation involved a new teacher who was not comfortable leading Option #4 with a disruptive and disrespectful student. I welcomed being asked to facilitate a mediation (Option #3) because I knew that this kind of modeling greatly increases comfort for being able to use Option #4 oneself.

Joey was a fourth grader with many problems. His mom no longer had custody of him, and he was living with his aunt. She cared a great deal for him, but he really wanted to be with his mom and was an angry child. Some of the problems Joey had at school included not paying attention during times of input, bothering other students (which included getting them off task and involved in disruptive behavior), angry outbursts (i.e., tipping over his desk and chair), using profanity, refusing to do what was asked, telling the teacher that he did not need to listen to him, and hiding in the restroom when it was time to come in from physical education.

Joey's teacher was just beginning to learn how to use the DTR Flowchart. He had been very pleased with our mediation that helped him meet with Joey and make an agreement that he thought would help not only Joey but also himself. He reported that the agreement helped immensely for the first two days, but then the old behavior began to happen again. We had planned our follow-up to happen in five days but we decided it would be better to meet as soon as possible. Arrangements were made for the hour after school when students remained in the after-school program. Joey was consulted about this, and he said he was willing to participate.

I was a little late joining Joey and his teacher. When I walked in Joey was completely turned around so that he was not facing his teacher. His teacher was talking to him in a calm voice but Joey's body language indicated that he was not listening. His teacher was glad to see me because he was concerned that the two of them were not accomplishing anything. I apologized for being late and asked Joey and his teacher if we could start the meeting over now that I had arrived. Joey said it would be okay if his teacher would stop saying the same things over and over. At this point I invited them to do some active listening with each other. We decided Joey would start. Once they actively listened to each other and Joey heard that his teacher understood that he had indeed been saying the same thing over and over, Joey turned around and was ready to work with his teacher. Joey's teacher (he is wonderfully open) verbally acknowledged that he had forgotten about active listening and apologized for repeating himself instead of using the process. They recommitted themselves to being constructive together. Since this situation is so complex, the following will provide some more background and detail regarding the mediated agreement before discussing the follow-up meeting.

Background and Summary of the Mediated Agreement

The agreement Joey and his teacher had made together included things that seem obvious. Joey agreed to stop distracting other students. It was arranged for him to have two places where he could sit. He had agreed to move himself to a place that was less public to the entire room when he was disturbing others. The agreement also said his teacher could ask him to move there if he did not realize he had started to bother other classmates. This would be done in a quiet, matter-of-fact voice. They had even practiced how this would look and sound so Joey would be able to distinguish that it was not meant to hurt or humiliate him but to help him and the rest of the class. Joey agreed that he would not tip over his desk or chair. They had talked about how dangerous this was to both him and others near him and how when things were dangerous his teacher needed to use Option #1 to make sure he and the others were safe. His teacher had told him he would prefer not to have to do this. We discussed that this meant Joey would need to leave the class and go to the Thinkery. Joey had agreed to stop and to go to the Thinkery quietly if he were doing things that were not safe. Again, the tone of voice was discussed, and we had a practice of what it would sound like if Joey needed to be sent to the Thinkery. Joey also agreed that it was important for him to listen to his teacher and to decide to do what his teacher asked him to do. He was assured that whatever his teacher asked him or the rest of the class to do was to help them all become better able to learn as they all prepared for their future lives. Finally, we came to the issue of hiding in the restroom. Joey said the only time he did this was when they had "free play" during their physical education period. He told us that when they had free play, he was sometimes unable to get a drink before they all had to go in. If he hid in the restroom, he would have the drinking fountain all to himself as soon as everyone else had gone in. However, he knew he would be in trouble if he went in late so he just kept hiding until his teacher got worried and called the office to send someone to look for him. It was decided that his teacher would blow his whistle ten minutes before it was time to go in and again when it was five minutes, so the whole class would know that it was almost time and could begin preparing by going more gradually to get their drinks. This would be explained to the entire class.

The Follow-up Meeting

I read the agreement that had been made and asked each of them how they were doing. Both agreed that the P.E. part of the agreement was going really well. Both agreed that Joey was keeping the agreement related to not doing things in class that were not safe. We celebrated this with positive words of affirmation that these parts of the agreement were going well.

The problems were with the other parts of the agreement. Joey acknowledged that his teacher was using the quiet tone of voice they had practiced, but he himself was not always keeping his part of the agreement of moving to his other desk if he was disrupting others. He liked moving on his own; it was the times that he needed to be asked to move that were the problem. On the first day, he had moved readily when asked. On the second day, he moved but he had to be asked more than once, and his teacher had been pretty worried that he was going to have a very angry outburst. Joey and his teacher agreed that this is what needed more thought and work.

We turned to figuring out how to work at this. I asked them if it would be helpful for them to each write a few ideas down on their own before talking about ideas. Joey wasn't sure he wanted to do this but changed his mind when he saw that his teacher was pretty enthused about doing this. I told Joey that he and I could do this together if he wanted, with me writing and him telling me what he wanted me to write. He liked this idea. He and I moved off to one side so we could do this without disturbing his teacher.

When we came back together (about five minutes later), each read his ideas. I wrote them on the whiteboard so we could see them. Joey had said he could move when he was asked to move. He also said he would like it better if he could move his second desk to another place so he would be able to see better. His teacher had also suggested Joey could move when he was asked to move and he, the teacher, would let Joey know he appreciated him each time by thanking him quietly when he moved on his own. Joey's teacher also wrote down that maybe he and Joey could talk to Joey's aunt to invite her to come to class to help Joey do what he was supposed to do if he was unable to keep the agreement for five days.

Joey and his teacher both liked all of these options except that Joey did not like the one that would have his aunt come to school to supervise him. Joey and his teacher agreed that they would not need to add that if Joey did what he agreed to do. We added the other new options to the agreement with Joey saying he would "try really hard." We discussed that "trying" usually sounded like people wanted to leave open the possibility that they would not keep the agreement. He said he would do more than try—he said he would keep the agreement.

We initialed the added agreements, and set a new follow-up time. We discussed the possibility of meeting in three days instead of five. Joey and his teacher agreed that this would be a good idea. I left as they began to figure out where Joey could move his second desk.

This follow-up meeting took us about forty-five minutes. The next follow-up meeting took about five minutes because we simply needed to affirm that the agreements were being kept with a few minor problems. We met again in five days. That was the last time we met. Joey and his teacher kept working together on their own.

Follow-up Meetings and Consequences

As illustrated in the story above, follow-up is a time to keep inviting cooperation and to keep valuing each other as problems are encountered and addressed. Each follow-up meeting, while focusing on the specific details related to the agreement, brings the focus back to the values of support, responsibility, and accountability. Sometimes teachers say, "It is not enough to just make agreements and keep them. The student should experience consequences." As you can see from these stories, each student was held accountable, accepted responsibility, and made significant changes. Rather than just "doing their time," they were learning and practicing significant life social skills. The consequences of these changes are enormous. The meetings themselves and the making and keeping of agreements are consequences. Making agreements with students is a choice that teachers make to use their power and authority as much as possible *with* students rather than *over* students. Agreements invite the change that is needed to help build relationships and the actions that are needed for maximum learning to occur. If students do not respond to this invitation, as indicated in the DTR Flow Chart, the teacher utilizes their power to constructively escalate the conflict by sending the student to the Thinkery (see Chapter 9).

An important requirement that teachers express related to classroom management is wanting students to learn to be respectful, accountable, and responsible. Agreements that are made, kept, and recognized as having been kept because of follow-up are certainly achieving these learning goals.

Chapter 9 • Thinkery

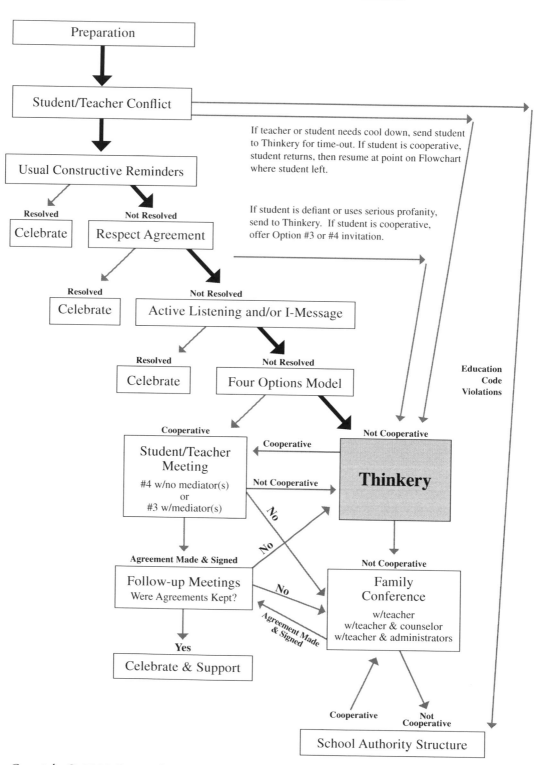

Preparation

Student/Teacher Conflict

Usual Constructive Reminders

If teacher or student needs cool down, send student to Thinkery for time-out. If student is cooperative, student returns, then resume at point on Flowchart where student left.

If student is defiant or uses serious profanity, send to Thinkery. If student is cooperative, offer Option #3 or #4 invitation.

Resolved — Celebrate

Not Resolved — Respect Agreement

Resolved — Celebrate

Not Resolved — Active Listening and/or I-Message

Resolved — Celebrate

Not Resolved — Four Options Model

Education Code Violations

Cooperative — Student/Teacher Meeting
#4 w/no mediator(s)
or
#3 w/mediator(s)

Cooperative

Not Cooperative — **Thinkery**

Not Cooperative

Not Cooperative

Agreement Made & Signed — Follow-up Meetings
Were Agreements Kept?

No

No

No

Agreement Made & Signed

Family Conference
w/teacher
w/teacher & counselor
w/teacher & administrators

Yes — Celebrate & Support

Cooperative

Not Cooperative

School Authority Structure

Copyright © 2008 Ron and Roxanne Claassen

Chapter 9
Thinkery

Introduction

What does a teacher do when a student does not respond to the invitations to cooperate? Each step of the DTR Flowchart is part of a constructive escalation inviting the student to choose to be cooperative and to work directly with the teacher to resolve problems/issues using Option #4 or #3. However, occasionally a student does not respond positively to these invitations. On the Flowchart, you will notice that there are arrows pointing to the right-hand side of the chart designed to address this infrequent situation. The arrows continue the constructive escalation by providing a Thinkery for the student who has refused to choose to be cooperative. The goal of the Thinkery is to encourage the student to decide to cooperate. The arrows move back and forth depending on whether or not each constructive escalation leads to cooperation. The Flowchart suggests that, in rare cases, one may need to refer an uncooperative student to the Thinkery early or at any point (perhaps because the teacher or student need time to cool down).

The Thinkery is for the occasional student who has refused all of the reminders and invitations to cooperate. The Thinkery is designed to help the student "think" about her or his refusal to cooperate. Usually this is done by talking with another adult about what he or she has been doing and experiencing along with its impact on the teacher and other students. It provides an opportunity for the student to reconsider his or her decision to refuse several invitations to cooperate. The Thinkery is used to continue the constructive escalation process.

You can see that as we move along the map of the DTR Flowchart, the teacher responses become more multifaceted because the conflict has escalated. We increase the pressure to work on a problem because the student has refused to cooperate to resolve the conflict, issue or misbehavior. As in other discipline plans, the more complicated things are also the things that are done the least frequently (meetings with parents, meetings with parents and administration, suspension, expulsion). We do not want students thinking they will be sent out of the room for any little thing. We want them to know we can and will work at those little things ourselves so they do not escalate and become the things that require them to leave the classroom. We want being sent out of the room to be something that helps students realize we are into some very serious territory here. We also want the purpose for their being sent out to be crystal clear.

The Thinkery is the place to send uncooperative students when they have refused the Usual Constructive Reminders, Respect Agreement reminder, I-message reminder, and the Four Options Model invitation, all of which take about thirty seconds. We use the Thinkery because there may be thirty-plus other students in class who want to learn without disruption. The Thinkery is where students who are not willing to cooperate are sent to have someone help them "think" about what happened and to consider their options. The student is not sent to the Thinkery for punishment.

Ron developed the idea for the Thinkery in 2003 as he worked with both Roxanne's school district and another one nearby on developing their restorative discipline plans. Here is what he says about the Thinkery:

- The student who refused to resolve the problem cooperatively (using the Conflict Resolution Option #4 or #3) is sent to the Thinkery.
- If a rule has been violated, the rule is identified and its purpose is explained. The student is invited to summarize.
- The student is asked to think about what happened by writing or talking about what happened. The adult in the Thinkery listens to and summarizes the student's concerns.
- The student is invited to reconsider working cooperatively with the teacher.
- The student is helped to think about, and perhaps even write, a plan to present to the teacher in a teacher/student meeting.
- If the student is uncooperative, the teacher proceeds to the next stop on the DTR Flowchart, Family Conference.

Roxanne's School Thinkery

Roxanne: As our teaching staff and I discussed instituting DTR, we concluded that there are times when it is helpful to the teacher and the other students for the student who is misbehaving to leave the room, especially if they are angry and refusing to cooperate. It was important that this be done in keeping with our own commitment to be constructive. We have found the Thinkery to be a constructive way to give the teacher, the other students in the class, and the uncooperative student a chance to continue a constructive escalation so that the problem will not be ignored and others are not kept from learning. There is also the possibility that time away enables the uncooperative student to reconsider and become willing to cooperate.

At my school, the Thinkery has been configured differently depending on the people resources available. At one time it was in a separate room (not the office) where a dean of students was available most of the time. At this time, we no longer have the luxury of a separate room with a dean. Now students are sent directly to the principal, who does the Thinkery process with each referred student. This increases accountability for all of us.

Students are sent to the Thinkery with a form designed to help them, along with the principal, to "think" about what was happening. The form is designed to help the uncooperative student accept responsibility for the behavior. It is not a place for the student to vent dissatisfaction with the teacher. The form asks the student to write a paragraph about the behavior that caused the referral to the Thinkery. It also asks the student to describe the impact the behavior has had on him or her, the teacher, and the other students. After discussing what the student has written, the principal again looks at the Flowchart and the Four Options Model and encourages the student to reconsider Option #4 or #3.

A Thinkery Story

Jesse arrived at school wearing a shirt that had gang-related symbols, which was against the dress code. The shirt was indicative of his uncooperative mood. I approached him as soon as possible about the shirt with a usual constructive reminder and then a respect agreement reminder. His response was, "That's all f***ed up. What's wrong with the shirt?" I composed an I-message on the spot (remembering my commitment to be constructive in spite of the anger I immediately felt). I said, "My reason for talking to you is that I cannot teach until I am sure all students are ready to learn. I feel confused when you wear such a shirt because it is against our dress code. I feel angry when you swear at me because that is against our respect agreement. I would prefer that you turn the shirt inside out or call your mom to bring you another shirt, and that you would not use profanity." Jesse's response was, "I'm not going to wear something inside out and I'm not going to call my mom."

We had a problem now on a number of levels. I referred to the Four Options Model and asked if he would be willing to do Option #4 with me. He refused Option #4 and insisted that there was nothing wrong with the shirt. He refused to make the adjustments that would allow him to stay in class. I told him that if he refused Option #4 he would need to leave class and go to the Thinkery. That was fine with him. I filled out the form (see Thinkery Form at the end of this chapter) and he went out of the room. This took about five minutes. While Jesse and I talked, the rest of the students got their books and prepared for literature. They knew we needed some space to work on this and were all highly cooperative.

Jesse left the room. He slammed his locker before he left, and I chose to ignore this. (There are some things we do have to ignore in order to get other important things done.) He was gone for about fifteen minutes, and returned to class with the Thinkery form filled out saying (happily for me) that he was willing to do an Option #4, a student/teacher meeting. His shirt was turned inside out, and he had called his mom, who was on her way with another shirt. As he handed me the form, he told me he was sorry for using the "f" word. I thanked him and said I was glad we would have the chance to talk more about the whole experience later. We decided to meet after school, since he was staying anyway for basketball practice. He got his books and sat down and was even more cooperative than usual. We met after school, and it went very well.

We will now focus on what the time in the Thinkery was like for Jesse. The dean calmly acknowledged him as he arrived with the Thinkery form. He took the form and asked Jesse to sit down to take a few moments to compose himself and to think while he read it. I had filled the form out by checking in the Reason for Referral section that the student was very upset, there was a rule violation, and he had refused all invitations to cooperate, including Option #4.

Jesse and the dean began by talking about the situation. He invited Jesse to write what they had talked about in the section "To Be Completed by the Student," which starts with this question: "What did I do to cause me to be referred to the Thinkery, and why is that a problem?" Jesse wrote, "I came to school wearing a gang shirt. I used the 'f' word when Mrs. Claassen asked me about keeping the respect agreement. It is a problem because the dress code says a shirt like the one I am wearing is not allowed and you are not supposed to swear at school."

The second question asks, "How did my behavior affect my teacher and/or other students?" Jesse (with some input from the dean) wrote, "She couldn't get class started because she had to talk to me. It didn't affect the others." This last sentence was crossed out and the following was put in its place after the dean asked if he was sure the others were not affected. "The class had to wait to get started because Mrs. Claassen was talking to me."

The third question asks, "What could I do differently in the future to prevent this referral?" Jesse wrote, "I could listen to the teacher and not cuss." The fourth question is: "After looking at the four options, am I willing to cooperate?" There is a box to check that says, "Meet with my teacher for Option #4" and another space that says, "If no, why not?" Jesse had indicated he was willing to meet with me.

After completing the form to this point, they discussed what Jesse needed to do regarding the shirt in order to return to class. Jesse told the dean I had said he could turn it inside out or call his mother to bring him another shirt. The dean asked him what he thought of these options. Jesse said he wanted to call his mom because he did not like the idea of wearing the shirt inside out all day—how he looked was very important to him. Jesse called his mom who was, luckily for him, at home and willing to bring him another shirt. The dean and Jesse then decided that if he would turn the shirt inside out while waiting for his mom to bring the shirt, he would be able to get back to class and not miss too much. Jesse decided that would be good since he knew his mom was not too happy with him at the moment (apparently they had a bit of a discussion on the phone when he called).

There were many reasons why the whole incident had happened as I learned from our student/teacher meeting. From the beginning of the year, I knew things were not going to be easy with Jesse, and I was thankful for the structure that was allowing us to keep working at things (the Peacemaking Process became very good news for Jesse). He was such a bright young man. I knew he had a lot to offer if he could develop some skills on his own that would enable him to be more willing to cooperate. This was not the only student/teacher meeting I had with him. The good news was that the structure kept inviting his cooperation and kept asking him to take responsibility in a way that valued and empowered him to do side-by-side problem solving. Ultimately he responded positively to this kind of invitation, although sometimes getting him to that point required going further along the Flowchart than with other students.

In the situation described here, there were invitations and consequences for Jesse, and those happened somewhat naturally. He decided, with the help of the structure that put him in the Thinkery (where he could get assistance), to turn his shirt inside out and to call his mother. Using the Flow Chart makes a big difference with a student who has developed habits of defiance.

Jesse's problems and habits did not change or disappear overnight. They had developed over a long period both at home and at school. He and I had several meetings. Some were very short and informal, and some were longer with formal, written agreements. Eventually we needed to proceed to a Family Conference, the next stop on the Flowchart (see Chapter 10). I am happy to say that Jesse did manage to make adjustments along the way that enabled him to graduate without ever being suspended. He and his parents were so grateful for this. They recognized that something different was being practiced, and they appreciated the support they felt as we worked together. One of my favorite pictures is one they took of me and Jesse together at graduation.

Thinkery Form Instructions

The Thinkery Form is designed to be a reminder to all involved of the importance of relationships and the choices that are made. The student needing to be sent from the classroom to the Thinkery is in need of additional help and support. The focus is on helping the student return to class where they will be welcomed back and will be ready to constructively participate in a learning environment that is supportive and conducive for learning and teaching for all members of the class. You are welcome to copy the Thinkery Form, or you can download it from the DTR Website: disciplinethatrestores.org

The Thinkery form is used when the teacher has tried several strategies to invite student cooperation and the student has refused to cooperate. The form is designed for the teacher to quickly fill in the first section of the form, "To be completed by the teacher," in order to refer an uncooperative student to the Thinkery. There, that student can think, with the help of another adult, about what they were doing that caused them to be referred to the Thinkery. When a teacher needs to make this kind of a referral, it usually means he or she and a student are in a power struggle (Option #1) which is causing a disturbance that is preventing learning for the rest of the students and is keeping the teacher from being able to teach.

The first section of the form is space for a number of preliminary items: the name of the student, the date, the name of the teacher, the room number, the time leaving the homeroom.

The "Reasons for referral" part of this section is designed to indicate the kind of conflict and if it is a possible educational code violation. The Student/Teacher part also helps the teacher record what invitations were offered to regain the cooperation of the disruptive student that the student refused. This is important for the teacher, the student, and the adult in the Thinkery. It is an important aspect of making a referral since having a student remain in class is so important for the maximum learning to occur. The teacher indicates whether or not she or he has offered a Usual Constructive Reminder, a Respect Agreement Invitation, Active Listening or an I-Message Invitation, and an Option #4 or #3 Invitation. These items can be checked off quickly as a reminder for the teacher to cover all these options and to inform the Thinkery adult of what has been offered to regain the cooperation of the student (this can be reviewed with the student). If the conflict is a Student/Student Conflict and the student has refused Peer Mediation, there is a space that can be checked for that. Finally there is a space for Possible Ed. Code Violation.

This first section is filled in and the form is given to the student, who is told to report to the Thinkery for time to think with another adult about what he or she is doing that is preventing him or her from being cooperative in the teaching/learning process. The spirit in which this is done is very important. The teacher will want to emphasize that the purpose of the Thinkery is to create the opportunity for the student to return to class as quickly as possible with a plan to resolve the "sending" issue and some ideas about how the problems can be worked on in the near future so the student can be restored to the classroom with the least amount of disturbance to learning.

When the student arrives at the Thinkery, the Thinkery adult (principal, vice principal, dean of students, psychologist, activity director are just a few ideas for who this person could be) reviews the first section of the form with the student and then uses the questions to guide a discussion to prepare the student for filling out the middle section of the form him- or herself. This second section is labeled: "To be competed by the student." The Thinkery adult uses this time to help the referred student think about their own actions (not the actions of others) that caused the referral. This can be very difficult for the student to do at first. A Thinkery adult is important because she or he can help the student focus on accepting responsibility for his or her actions rather than making excuses.

When the Thinkery adult and the student decide the student is ready, the student answers questions one to four. Questions one to three are designed to help the student reflect on what happened, how his or her actions affected others, and what he or she could do differently to be a successful learner in the classroom. Question four is designed to help the student decide and indicate willingness (or unwillingness) to cooperate.

If no Thinkery outside the classroom is available, it is possible for the form to be used within the classroom with a designated location for the student to fill out the form. In order for this to work, students would need to be very well informed about the purpose and process of Discipline That Restores so they would know how to use the form and would be willing to cooperate enough to separate themselves and fill in the form seriously. Sometimes the short timeout that this provides is very effective in regaining the cooperation of a student.

When the student in the Thinkery has filled in the student section of the form, the Thinkery adult looks at the form with the student. The student will have indicated under number four whether or not she or he is willing to cooperate with the teacher at #4 or #3, or, if it is a student/student conflict, with peer mediators. If the student is still not ready to cooperate, he or she will write down the reasons.. The Thinkery adult can then talk with the student about the choices made.

The last section of the form, "To be completed by Thinkery adult," provides a space to indicate the time the student arrived at the Thinkery, and the time the student leaves to return to the classroom.

The Thinkery adult indicates if the student has chosen to cooperate with a #4, #3, or Peer Mediation. If the student has agreed to cooperate, the option the student has chosen is checked, and she or he are ready to return, with the form, to the classroom. If the student has chosen #4, it is very important for the teacher to arrange a time to sit down with the student to work at an agreement. If the student has chosen #3, the Thinkery adult will help arrange for that mediation. The Thinkery adult will refer the student to the Peer Mediation program if the student has indicated that option. If the student has refused to work at #4 or #3, the Thinkery adult will arrange for a family conference before sending the student back to class. There is a space for the Thinkery adult to refer the student to other resources for additional help if that is what he or she chooses. Finally, there is a space for suspension due to violation of the educational code. If a student is suspended, a #3 meeting is arranged before the student is readmitted to the classroom.

Thinkery Form

To be completed by the Teacher:

Student Name: _____ Date: _____

Teacher: _____ Room#: _____

Time leaving homeroom: _____ Time returning to homeroom: _____

Reason for referral:

_____ Student/Teacher Conflict. Student Refused to Cooperate:
     _____ Usual Constructive Reminder
     _____ Respect Agreement Invitation
     _____ I-Message/Active Listening Invitation
     _____ Option #4 Invitation.

_____ Student/Student Conflict. Refused Peer Mediation.

_____ Possible Ed. Code Violation

To be completed by the student:

1. What did I do to cause me to be referred to the Thinkery? Why is that a problem?

   _____
   _____
   _____

2. How did my behavior affect my teacher and/or other students?

   _____
   _____
   _____

3. What could I do differently in the future to prevent this referral?

   _____
   _____
   _____

4. After looking at the four options, I am willing to cooperate:
   With my teacher at #4. _____ Yes _____ No Or With my teacher at #3 _____ Yes _____ No
   With Peer Mediation _____ Yes _____ No
   If no, why not? _____

To be completed by Thinkery adult:

Student arrived: _____ Student left the Thinkery at: _____

1. _____ Student has agreed to work with you at #4.

2. _____ Student has agreed to work with you at #3. I will help arrange for a mediation.

3. _____ Student has agreed to be referred to the Peer Mediation Program.

4. _____ Student has refused to work at #4 or #3 so I will arrange for a Family Conference before sending him/her back to class. I will let you know when.

5. _____ Student has been referred to _____ for additional help.

6. _____ Student has been Suspended due to violation of Ed Code #_____.
   Upon their return I will arrange a #3 meeting before readmitting him/her to the classroom.

Copyright © 2008 Ron and Roxanne Claassen

Chapter 10 • **Family Conference**

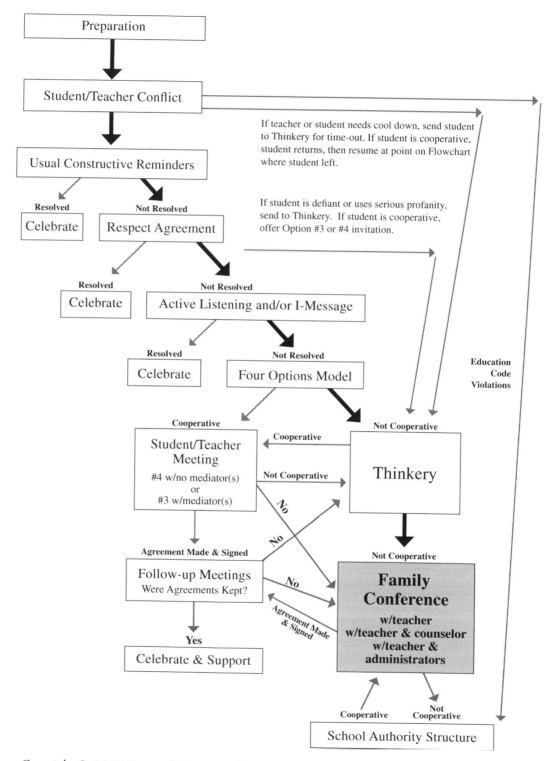

Preparation

Student/Teacher Conflict

If teacher or student needs cool down, send student to Thinkery for time-out. If student is cooperative, student returns, then resume at point on Flowchart where student left.

Usual Constructive Reminders

If student is defiant or uses serious profanity, send to Thinkery. If student is cooperative, offer Option #3 or #4 invitation.

Resolved
Celebrate

Not Resolved
Respect Agreement

Resolved
Celebrate

Not Resolved
Active Listening and/or I-Message

Resolved
Celebrate

Not Resolved
Four Options Model

Education Code Violations

Cooperative
Student/Teacher Meeting
#4 w/no mediator(s)
or
#3 w/mediator(s)

Cooperative

Not Cooperative
Thinkery

Not Cooperative

No

No

Agreement Made & Signed
Follow-up Meetings
Were Agreements Kept?

No

Not Cooperative
Family Conference
w/teacher
w/teacher & counselor
w/teacher & administrators

Agreement Made & Signed

Yes
Celebrate & Support

Cooperative

Not Cooperative

School Authority Structure

Copyright © 2008 Ron and Roxanne Claassen

Chapter 10
Family Conference

Introduction

Family members have the greatest influence on a student and can be wonderful allies to the teacher and school. When invited into a constructive process to address the issues of a misbehaving student, family members welcome the help, support and accountability of a family conference.

A Family Conference is convened when all of the prior reminders and invitations, including the Thinkery, have failed to gain the cooperation of the student. The purpose of this stop on the DTR Flowchart is to gather the family of the student in order to work on the issues and to gain the student's cooperation. This stop on the Flowchart continues the constructive escalation of the conflict in order to keep working constructively with a student to invite cooperation in a way that promotes learning while not disrupting the learning of those students who are cooperative.

The Family Conference, as described on the Flowchart, is not intended to suggest that a teacher shouldn't have contact with a student's family outside this formal structure. We think that it is very is valuable for a teacher to develop a positive relationship with a family. When there is a prior positive relationship between the teacher and the family, it will serve to make this formal family conference even more effective.

This stop on the Flowchart is important because a student has refused all of the other attempts to gain his or her cooperation. Remember, this stop is rarely needed. One's commitment to be constructive is very important at every stop on the Flowchart and especially as we move into these escalated situations where issues are more serious and emotions are heightened. You will be using the Family Conference stop with your most difficult and challenging students. Remember Roxanne's earlier comment, "Students who need love the most deserve it the least."

Here is how Ron has described what happens when parent contact needs to be made to arrange a family conference. For purposes of making this as clear as possible, the family conference is discussed here as Level 1 and Level 2. A Level 1 Family Conference is convened by the teacher when a student has refused to participate in a student/teacher meeting or has repeatedly not kept agreements made in student/teacher meetings. A Level 1 conference includes the teacher, the student, and the parents of the student. A Level 2 conference is convened when the agreements made in a Level 1 conference are not being kept or if the issues include serious safety concerns. A Level 2 conference includes the above people and school administration.

Family Conference Level 1: Parents, Student, Teacher

- Parents are contacted by the teacher and invited to help their child consider resolving the problem cooperatively at a family conference or to encourage their student to return to a student/teacher meeting.
- If the student does not return to the student/teacher meeting, a family conference is convened. This meeting includes the student, parents, and the teacher (possibly also Thinkery person or counselor).
- The meeting is led by the teacher (making it an Option #4), or a conflict resolution specialist or the Thinkery person using a mediation process (making it Option #3).
- The group follows the Peacemaking Process (see Chapter 7).
- The group writes and signs the agreements made to resolve the problem.
- Follow-up meetings are held to assess if the agreements are working, to make modifications if desired, to schedule additional follow-up meetings, and/or to celebrate agreements that have been kept. If agreements are repeatedly not being kept or if the issues have escalated, proceed to a Family Conference Level 2.

Family Conference Level 2: Parents, Student, Teacher, Vice Principal, Principal (or whatever administration fulfills this role)

- Teacher meets with administration to inform them of the attempts to gain cooperation, the refusals or agreements not kept, and the need for a Family Conference Level 2.
- Parents are contacted by administration and invited to help their child resolve the problem cooperatively (#3 or #4) in Family Conference Level 2.

- The group reviews the history, starting with the attempts to gain cooperation, a review of the problematic behavior, and any rule violations.
- The reasons behind the DTR Flowchart and the rules are explained and discussed.
- The group, following the Peacemaking Process, seeks to arrive at a cooperative agreement that restores equity and clarifies future intentions.
- The group writes and signs agreements made to resolve the problem.
- Follow-up meetings are held to assess if the agreements are working, to make modifications if desired, to schedule additional follow-up meetings, and/or to celebrate agreements that have been kept.
- If the conference does not arrive at a cooperative agreement (Option #3 or #4), the administration informs the student and parents that the situation will be addressed by the school authority structure (Option #2). The administrator explains that this is not intended to hurt or punish, but to encourage the student to cooperate. The administered consequence is not an alternative to cooperation because before the student is readmitted to class, she or he will have to come to an agreement with the teacher.

A few stories will help to illustrate the structure and process of a family conference. While each situation is unique and takes its own direction, the structures and strategies of the family conference keep the participants on track for as much restoration as possible given all of the difficult circumstances each situation presents. Below, Roxanne will share two of her experiences with family conferences. The first story is a Level 1 situation, and the second is a Level 2.

A Family Conference Story—Level 1

Roxanne: Eighth-grader Jessica was not doing her homework. We went through the steps of the Flowchart rather quickly. The result of our student/teacher meeting was an agreement that acknowledged Jessica's ability to get grades of C on tests even without her completing her homework. The agreement also acknowledged how much better she could do if she put in the time rereading and doing assignments designed to give her a much deeper understanding of concepts. We also discussed the fact that some of her Cs were very close to being Ds. Things improved for a week, and then she slipped back into the habit of not doing the homework. In our agreement, we had decided that if follow-up showed she was not getting her work done, we would have a meeting with her, her mom, and me. It was time to have this meeting.

I talked to Jessica's mother on the telephone. Jessica had told her I would be calling. Her mom had also been concerned about Jessica. Jessica had been telling her that her work was done in school or that she didn't have homework whenever her mom asked her if she needed to get her homework done. Her mom did not believe this could be possible at the eighth-grade level, but she had taken her daughter's word for it anyway. Jessica's mother was not interested in talking to Jessica about this and then having Jessica and me repeat another student/teacher meeting. She wanted to sit down as soon as possible with her daughter and me. We arranged the meeting for the next day after school.

This was an Option #4 with me acting as the leader for the meeting as well as being a participant. We agreed that we would use the Peacemaking Process. Each person described how she experienced the problem and chose who would summarize. It was interesting that Jessica's mom chose Jessica to summarize. This summary was very difficult for Jessica as she internalized the level of disappointment her mother was experiencing. When each person said that her experience had been recognized, we turned to making things right. Jessica apologized for her behavior and her lying (this was a very emotional time). We acknowledged her apologies. We also recognized that our hurt was connected to the fact that she was the person who was getting hurt by the behavior, and we cared about her. We then focused on some additional things for making things right between us and making agreements for the future that would prevent the problem from reoccurring. We each wrote what we thought needed to be done to make things right and what needed to be done so this behavior would not continue. Our lists included making apologies, doing what was needed to be prepared for class, figuring out a schedule that included some free time, getting better grades, a desire not to have to carry heavy books home, putting ideas into place so Jessica could reach the goals she had for herself, giving Jessica time to read whatever she wanted to read, and Jessica being willing to approach her studies in a more serious way so she could fulfill her potential. We decided as we looked at the lists that Jessica could make things right and prevent this from happening again in the future if we were creative.

The agreement we developed included a schedule that Jessica would keep each day after school that gave her time for doing chores, doing homework, talking to friends, watching TV, and reading whatever she wanted to read. The agreement for the future also included Jessica's mom calling me (I had said I preferred this to my needing to think of making the call) each Tuesday for the first three weeks to see how things were going and for getting an idea of how the week's assignments would look. This was needed because trust had been lost. As we discussed options related to carrying heavy books, it was decided Jessica would simply continue using the backpack she had since she did not like the idea of getting something that had wheels (no one else in the eighth grade used such a case), and she did not want to commit to staying for an hour after school to get things done that required a book to be carried home. Jessica basically decided this was not as big an issue as she had thought.

We did the follow-up meeting as we had scheduled it. After three weeks, we recognized that all of us were keeping all of the agreements and Jessica was taking care of things related to homework on her own. When she saw her grades improve, she really seemed ready to be independent and on her own related to this issue. This was a built-in kind of celebration. Her mom was so happy they also celebrated by going out for pizza. We did not need any further meetings to resolve anything related to Jessica.

A Family Conference Story — Level 2

Roxanne: Carlos, Noe, Maria, and Blanca left class each morning at ten to meet with Mrs. Johnson for an intense hour of English language acquisition. The boys were often laughing, joking, and teasing the girls. All was well until Mrs. Johnson began to notice that the girls were angry about the teasing. She asked them about it. They said Carlos and Noe had begun to say bad things to them in Spanish that they did not like. Mrs. Johnson talked to the boys. They denied that they were saying bad things. They were just teasing the girls and having fun. They said they would stop. However, it became clear that they did not stop, and they became bolder in their teasing.

Mrs. Johnson talked to the boys again. She showed them where they were on the Flowchart and told them that since they had not stopped on their own, she wanted to have a meeting with them, the girls, and me (their classroom teacher) where we would formally discuss what was happening and get the problem solved using the Peacemaking Process. After looking at the Four Options Model and her suggesting a #3 with me leading the meeting, they agreed.

I led the student/teacher meeting using the Peacemaking Process. Because of the structure of the meeting, the boys became accountable for what they had been saying. The presence of the girls and their willingness to say what had been happening and the boys needing to summarize what they said caused them to take responsibility. An agreement was written and signed that recognized the injustices, made things as right as possible, and declared their constructive intentions for the future. The agreement also included that parents would be informed since this was a very serious rule violation. Noe and Carlos were not thrilled about this but they agreed to it. The girls had already been talking with their parents. It was a good agreement and a follow-up meeting was scheduled.

At the follow-up meeting it became clear the boys were not keeping their part of the agreements. Things had improved at first but were quickly returning to pre-agreement behavior. The boys recognized this and recommitted themselves to keeping the agreement.

The next time the girls complained to her about this, Mrs. Johnson sent the boys to the Thinkery. Carlos and Noe came out of the Thinkery willing to return to the student/teacher meeting. However, the dean wanted to be part of this meeting due to the seriousness of this rule violation. I again acted as the mediator. At this meeting, which included only the boys, the dean, and me, we went over the agreements Carlos and Noe had made and not kept. We discussed the seriousness of what they were doing. Sexual harassment is a state education code violation and clearly not allowed at school. We suggested that it was time we meet with them and their parents so they could get the help and support they needed to understand what they were doing. They also needed to take responsibility and stop the behavior, because it was serious enough that if they continued they would not be allowed to stay at school. They agreed reluctantly to this. Either way, they knew their parents would again be informed. A family conference seemed like a better option to them since both knew their parents thought school was very important and would not want to see them suspended or expelled. We also let the boys know that Maria and Blanca's parents needed to know what had been happening since our original mediation so they could help their daughters with the bad feelings they were experiencing because of what the boys were saying to them. As the boys summarized this, the boys began to fully understand the seriousness of their actions. We suggested that Maria and Blanca's parents might also wish to be part of the meetings so they would also be assured of the future and that their daughters were safe.

The girls had been keeping their parents informed. At our meeting between them and the boys, it had been decided that the girls would show their parents copies of our agreement from our mediation meeting. When I talked with the girls' parents about the family conference, both sets of parents expressed appreciation for what was happening and said they did not feel they or their daughters needed to be at the meeting with the boys and their parents. They said they would appreciate seeing the results of this next meeting, the family conference. I believe the parents were seeing that the concerns of the girls were being addressed and not dismissed as unimportant. Sometimes parents feel helpless when their child tells them of a school concern. They might tell their child to stay away from the people causing the problem but they know that may not help. They might also want the boys to be punished, but they also know that might not help. These parents appreciated what was happening.

We arranged to have a separate family conference with each of the boys. Each conference would include the boy, his parents, the dean, the principal, Mrs. Johnson, and me as the mediator. The family conferences happened separately with each boy and his parents following the Peacemaking Process; however, since they were very similar they are discussed here together. I began each meeting by sharing what each boy had written about respect (at the beginning of the year while developing the respect agreement) and their goals (also part of the beginning of the year process). I assured the parents in each meeting that I knew they had done what they needed to do to teach their sons right from wrong. Both sets of parents greatly appreciated this and let us know they were appalled and disappointed in what their sons had been saying to the girls (by this time the boys had honestly told their parents what was happening in preparation for these meetings). We went through the process, giving each boy a chance to say exactly what it was he had been saying and doing. Each set of parents (both dads and moms were there) summarized. Then it was the turn of the parents to tell their son how they experienced this and that this was not how they wanted their family to be known. This was very emotional and difficult for the boys to summarize and it was clear that the results of their "teasing" words were finally getting through to them. This was not simple and fun teasing. This was very serious, and no one saw it as fun.

Next we discussed what would need to be done to make things as right as possible and what would need to be done to ensure that this would not continue in the future. New agreements were made in which the boys again agreed not to speak to the girls the way they had been. This may seem simple and obvious, but we were aware that the obvious was not that simple since we were now in a serious meeting with the dean, the principal, each boy, and each set of parents. The agreement included having the boys write an apology to each of the girls with the help of their parents. A follow-up meeting was scheduled where we would all sit down again to see if the agreements were being kept. Each of these meetings took about forty-five minutes.

Our first follow-up was a week after the agreements were made. The apologies had been written and given to the girls, who were very forgiving. This meeting took about fifteen minutes. Our next follow-up was set up for a month later. At that meeting, we decided we would meet only if there were more problems. Agreements were being kept, things were going very well and the four students felt friendly toward one another and safe. The boy's parents felt a sense of pride that their boys were behaving the way they had taught them to behave and they had made things as right as possible. We celebrated that we would not need the next step where consequences needed to be imposed. Each of these final follow-up meetings took about twenty minutes.

Reflections on a Family Conference

What happened here? Structures and strategies were used that took the problem very seriously and also made sure all of the parties felt each one was of infinite value to all of us as people. This was a teachable moment for Carlos and Noe as well as Maria and Blanca, Mrs. Johnson, the parents of the boys, the dean, the principal, and me. We all learned a great deal about understanding one another, right and wrong, responsibility and accountability, making and keeping agreements, and the way that enables trust to grow once again. The process restored everyone to the community. A punishment process might have left Carlos and Noe isolated and without hope for being able to develop new patterns of relating to persons of the opposite sex. This would have led them into deeper trouble rather than helping them out of trouble.

The time this took was time very well spent. It left Mrs. Johnson and me energized because we could see that learning and progress were occurring. I would estimate that all of this took a total of three hours. Other types of structures take time as well, not to mention the emotional stress that is caused when sending a child out of the room or away from school for a while, but do not deal with any of the issues or learning the child needs to experience. If it leads to dealing with angry parents, even more emotional stress is experienced and the problem may still not be resolved. My experience has also been that needing to go this far on the Flowchart is rare. While all of this happens as privately as possible, it still acts as a deterrent for other students as they see that all types of misbehavior will be taken very seriously.

The use of the DTR Flowchart led to better understanding among us, rather than alienation and no understanding. It led to changed behavior rather than repeated misbehavior that gets worse and worse as the relationships deteriorate. I did not have to dread the day Noe and Carlos would return to class wanting to prove they were unbothered by being ever more abusive in their language and behavior. Instead, our relationship became positive and respectful, and I enjoyed seeing them enter the classroom each morning. The type of conference we had clearly put the burden on the boys to make changes and be accountable. They had a part in deciding what they would do to make things right rather than the adults imposing a contract on them in which they had no say. The process of detentions/suspension/expulsion is also very time consuming, requiring contacts, documentation, and meetings that are often not satisfying if the behavior worsens.

The story of Noe and Carlos ended with them being cooperative so there was no further need of the school authority structure, which is the last stop on the Flowchart. It is rare, but there are times that the school authority structure is needed. This will be discussed in the next chapter.

Chapter 11 • **School Authority Structure**

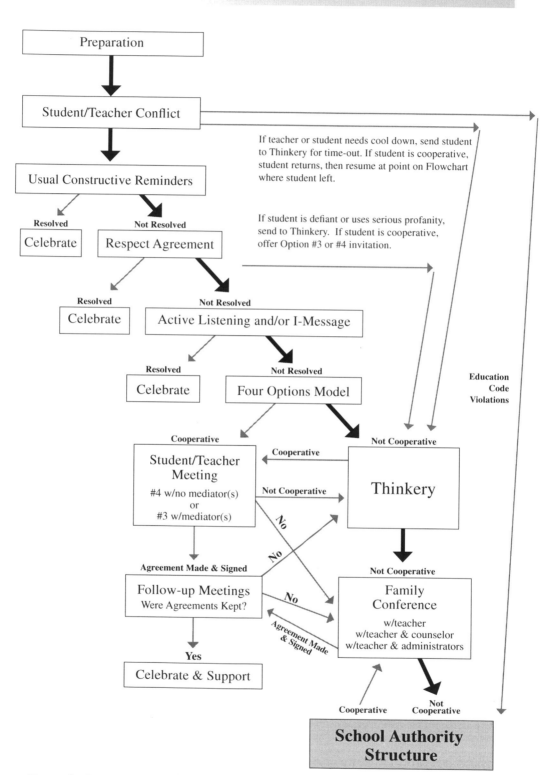

Copyright © 2008 Ron and Roxanne Claassen

Chapter 11
School Authority Structure

Introduction

The school rules and authority structure are necessary for the purpose of keeping students as safe as possible while they are at school. In a DTR structure, the rules and authority are certainly still necessary and available if a student or students refuse to cooperate. Refusal to cooperate presents dangers for the uncooperative student as well as for others on a school campus. These dangers can include physical, academic, and psychological harm. When the school authority structure is utilized, it should still only be in ways that are respectful, reasonable, and restorative and, when possible, reintegrative.

If the student has a good understanding of the Four Options, he or she will recognize the use of this structure as an Option #2 or #1 with the school authority being inside of the circle. The student has made a decision not to participate in the making or keeping of agreements. The student has decided, in a sense, to give up her or his authority over her- or himself and turn it over to others who will make the decisions. We are not sure what leads a student to seek this option. We do know that there are times when that is what a student seems to want. It is as if they genuinely need someone else to be in control of them for a time. Sometimes it is entering this authority structure that helps a student determine this is not what he or she wants after all, and the student decides to cooperate. When this happens, we go back on the DTR Flowchart to the Family Conference. Parents are present and involved anyway when the authority structures need to be used.

Roxanne has experienced two situations in the last eighteen years where students and their parents decided that the students would voluntarily seek to enter another school. Here is the story of one of those situations.

School Authority Structure Story

Roxanne: This story happened at a time when DTR was being considered by the administration and only partially embraced. (I believe that it would be a very different story if the same situation developed today.) I decided to tell the story because it illustrates a situation in which the student refused all of the invitations to cooperate with me. I believe that our relationship was negatively impacted by things that happened outside my classroom that did not follow the DTR criteria of applying the school authority. More recently, we experienced a situation that could have escalated similarly, but when the school authority structure followed the DTR process, the students decided to return to the family conference, agreements were made and they were kept.

Efren was a student who moved around from school to school. This was often due to his being expelled. He had been in and out of our school several times. He was having a fairly good experience with us in seventh grade, and was back at our school again after having been expelled in fifth grade (pre-DTR) for a fight that had left the other child bloodied and scared. The seventh-grade teacher and I worked closely together using the structures and strategies described in this book. Efren's problems in seventh grade happened more outdoors than in the classroom itself. In the classroom, he was cooperative with his teacher, who was using the DTR Flowchart process. But, due to concerns about some rough behavior outside, the administration decided and announced to Efren, his parents, and his teacher that Efren was to be put on home studies for the last six weeks of school.

Efren's teacher carefully prepared the lessons he would need to complete at home. He was to be in seventh grade again if he did not complete the work and did not follow through with the meetings that would oversee the completion and correction of the work. This imposed contract was not honored. The teacher did not see Efren at all during this time, because his parents did not bring him to the scheduled meetings. His teacher thought perhaps they had made other arrangements. It is difficult to supervise a student in this situation. I was not part of these decisions and knew very little about the situation at this point. (This story would be different if it were to happen today. At the time of this story, while there was significant commitment to the Flowchart, it was not as strong as it is today.)

Efren showed up at our school the next school year and was enrolled in eighth grade (my class) by his parents. The office had no idea there had been arrangements made the year before that might prevent this. So Efren started the year in my class.

He participated in writing his goals, which were constructive goals like other students. He participated actively in developing the respect agreement and signed it along with the other students. Using this structure, he got along quite well in the classroom and did quite well in his academics.

Our problems in the classroom started after he was responded to on the playground and in the cafeteria with Option #1s that he did not consider fair. I was not aware of this and became concerned as he became less cooperative in our classroom. In conversations with the seventh-grade teacher, I discovered that there had been an arrangement made near the end of the year for him to be on home studies to allow him to complete the last six weeks of his seventh grade assignments or to enroll in another school. The understanding was that successful completion of one of these options would determine which grade he would enter. As I began checking into the situation, it became clear Efren had not completed the assignments and he had not gone to another school to finish the year. Unaware of this prior arrangement, office staff assigned him to eighth grade. When I reflect on what happened in regard to this arrangement not being completed and Efren being allowed into the eighth grade, it turned out to be Option #1 with Efren and his parents in the circle.

When I discussed with administration the fact that Efren did not complete the arrangement from the last year, the administration decided that since he was performing well in class and he was old enough, it did not really seem to be in the best interest of anyone to put him back in seventh grade. Unfortunately, this decision was not made with Efren, his parents, or me. Once again Option #1 was used to make a decision.

About the ninth week of school, Efren got into a fight on the playground and was suspended for seven days (another Option #1). The class came in from lunch break and he was not there. I asked if anyone knew where he was. Students told me he had been sent to the office. I called the office, and they told me Efren was suspended. His mom came to the school and asked for the work that he would miss. I gave it to her, hoping this would keep him from getting too far behind.

Efren arrived back at school after the seven days with no work done, dressed inappropriately, with a belligerent, uncooperative attitude, and angry. I was on the receiving end of a lot of accumulated anger. He did agree to adjust his sagging pants and remove the cap he was wearing. However, when the algebra assignment was given, he refused to do the work when it was time for students to practice on their own. It was clear he hadn't done any of the assignments while he was gone. I suggested I could help him if he would be willing to go back to the assignments he had missed because an understanding of that would help him with the current concepts. He refused.

I reminded myself of my commitment to be constructive. I showed Efren his goals, which he had written the first day of school where he had indicated his desire to make good progress in school. Then, following the steps of the Flowchart, I offered usual reminders, and a respect agreement invitation, He refused all of these. He finally yelled that he wanted to be left alone; he didn't want to do anything. I used active listening to summarize. With an I-message I told him I could not simply leave him alone and allow him to do nothing. He had been gone for seven days and if we did not get started right away on catching him up, he would get too far behind for it to be possible to catch up. I would prefer that we would do an Option #4. He swore at me. I filled out a Thinkery form. He took it and his backpack and went to see the dean.

When he returned, he announced in a singsong voice, "I'm back." The pants were sagging once again (he had made a stop at the restroom after leaving the dean), he had the cap, which had been put in his backpack, on crooked, and it was clear he was not planning to cooperate. The form had been completed but not in a way that showed he was going to take responsibility. In fact, it was checked that he was unwilling to meet with me and he had been assigned a detention by the dean. If we had followed the Flowchart, the dean would have arranged for a family conference and not returned him to class until that was completed and new agreements were in place. I filled out a second Thinkery form and sent him back to the dean. The dean called his parents and sent him home with the arrangement that he would be welcome to return when the assignments were done and he was dressed properly. The dean then informed me of what he had done. Unfortunately this was another Option #1 instead of what should have been a family conference.

He did not return for three days. When he did return, he was simply waiting by the door as if nothing had happened. I asked to see his completed assignments. He had no work. I told him I understood the arrangement was he could not return to class until the work was complete and he was willing to cooperate in an Option #4 or #3 with me. I sent him back to the dean. As he walked over, I called the dean to request a family conference (Level 2), a meeting with Efren, his parents, and the administration. The dean consulted with the principal. They called Efen's parents right away, and a meeting was set up for noon with all of us. Efren remained with the dean until the meeting. I simply felt it was unfair to me and especially the rest of the class to have him present in the room not knowing what he was going to do or say. I appreciated the support I received from both the dean and the principal at this point.

At the noon meeting, Efren continued to refuse to cooperate. He would not talk and participate. Given his refusal to cooperate, we (dean, principal, parents, and me) looked at options that included putting Efren on home studies or going to a different school where it might be possible to get a new start that did not involve his needing to save face by continuing to be uncooperative. It was clear to his parents that we would not simply allow him to be back with no signs of cooperation. I had the chance to say how unfair it felt since the initial problem that got him suspended had nothing to do with me and our relationship, but now, somehow, that was where all of Efren's anger was being focused.

We gave Efren and his parents the chance to talk privately. When we all reconvened, they said they were voluntarily going to remove him from our school and enroll him someplace else. This is what they did. I let Efren know that I was sad that this was what was going to happen and that I also wished him well as he moved on.

I would have preferred for Efren to decide to cooperate. I would have worked with him for a long time if he had been willing to take some steps to improve his behavior. Such behavior is not going to end immediately. It usually takes time and small steps toward change. I was sad that he was moving on and that we would not have the chance to work it out together. I was also glad that he was moving on because this meant an uncooperative person would not be a danger to the others. The rest of the class could get on with their academic goals without disruption. The family conference together with the final steps of authority structure worked well. Had we needed to wait for him to leave until he had accumulated some large number of misbehaviors, far more time would have been spent dealing with the situation and far more stress would have been experienced by Efren, the class, and me.

I have seen Efren around the community several times since all of this occurred, and we were able to talk about how the rest of the year went for him and what he was doing currently. If things had not ended reasonably, respectfully, and restoratively, he and I would probably have avoided speaking. Our being able to meet by chance and talk amicably shows that the above criteria were met toward the end of this story even as we used the authority structure that was in place for those who refuse to cooperate.

I include this story because it illustrates that the Flowchart does address even the most serious misbehavior. The earlier story of Carlos and Noe is much more the norm when the Flowchart is followed earlier and throughout to the end of the problem. The authority structure was involved only to escalate the situation to the point that the boys were willing to take responsibility for their behavior and modify it in a way that enabled them to remain at school. I have no examples where the Flowchart structure was followed throughout the problem where a student had to or chose to leave the school.

Embedding Restorative Discipline in Structure

Ron: Most classroom and school discipline systems have goals that are restorative. However, discipline structures vary widely in how to accomplish the restorative goals. At Fresno Pacific University, our student discipline goals had been stated in restorative terms for many years. Nevertheless, when we examined our structure, it was a punitive structure. We asked the same three questions as punitive discipline systems: Was a rule violated? Who did it? And how should he or she be punished? A restorative discipline system asks different questions. Was a rule violated? What are the needs and obligations created by the violation? And how could things be made as right as possible? Since structure exerts a great force on those who are both the ones administering it as well as those who are governed by it, the force of the structure overcomes the goals if they are not pulling in the same direction.

When restorative justice is embedded in a school's structure along with restorative goals, the results are consistently positive. We have focused this book on Roxanne's experience at Raisin City School and the development and implementation of a restorative discipline structure that we have called Discipline That Restores (see handbook copy at www.disciplinethatrestores.org). The positive experience of Raisin City School is not unique. Hundreds of teachers who have adopted DTR have reported similar experiences. Two other examples of schools embedding restorative discipline in their structures are Fresno Pacific University and Immanuel High School in Reedley, California.

Restorative discipline has been in place at Fresno Pacific University for two full years now. (Ron introduced Restorative Discipline at FPU and continues to help implement it. See www.disciplinethatrestores.org for an article that describes the development and first year of implementation.) During that time, only one situation each year has progressed to an authority structure, and in each case this was requested by the student. (See www.fresno.edu/sharedmedia/studentlife/restorativediscipline.pdf for a complete description of the Restorative Discipline policy manual.

Chapter 12
Conclusion: Obstacles and Opportunities

We want to conclude with the recognition of some obstacles you may already be thinking about as you consider adding to and changing your way of working at conflicts with your students. Our purpose for recognizing the obstacles is to encourage you in your process of implementation. Obstacles, just as all conflicts, present us with dangers and opportunities.

Change

Most of us have a natural resistance to change. Change of job, of address, of marital status—even good change—has been shown to increase the stress we feel in our everyday lives. The DTR Flowchart may be asking you to change some ways of reacting and responding to students in times of conflict. Students may themselves resist this change even if it is in the direction of bringing out the opportunities our conflicts present for better understanding between us. Eventually ways will be found to cope with new situations, and these new ways sometimes so thoroughly replace the old ways that the old ways are not even remembered. Be willing to give yourself time as you implement DTR to experience the new and positive directions the structure will encourage. Allow yourself to learn from your mistakes. Mistakes are often the points at which the most learning occurs. At these points, be willing to look back at the theory and ideas for the implementation of the structure and try it again.

Time

Time is the obstacle that is perhaps mentioned first and most often when teachers learn of these strategies. You may be asking, "How do I get the time to go through the stops on the Flowchart, plus teach my students all the other things they must know?" Roxanne has found that using the DTR strategies takes no more time (and she thinks even less) than using other discipline strategies. Time will be spent in figuring out what to do in a classroom community when there is misbehavior and then working on that with students whether you practice this structure or some other structure. When one first sees the Flowchart, it often looks a little overwhelming and time consuming. However, if you put what you already do on a Flowchart, you may find it looking even more complicated and overwhelming and/or you may find that you are already doing part of the DTR system. Following the Flowchart is both efficient and effective. Because the DTR strategy is a continuation of your teaching time, you are actually diverted less from teaching when following the Flowchart.

Discipline simply takes time. It is important that the time spent is productive, changes the way a student responds, and teaches the student whatever he or she needs to learn about being a constructive member in a community. Our experience and the research indicate that, when provided good instruction and restorative discipline, most students do what is positive for themselves and others around them. The first several stops on the DTR Flowchart, Usual Constructive Reminders and the development and use of the Respect Agreement, are designed to teach, encourage, and support all students in being constructive members of a community. The later steps on the Flowchart (Thinkery and Family Conference) are effective and efficient strategies that continue teaching civility, responsibility, and accountability for those who need more assistance with these.

Utilizing the DTR Flowchart allows a teacher to provide life-giving attention for all students. Time spent in producing constructive outcomes is time well spent.

Sharing Power and the Fear of Permissiveness

Leaders who consider moving from Option #1 to Option #4 on the Four Options Model often report that they feel like they are moving from inside the circle in #1 to outside the circle in #1. They may think/feel they are giving up their power. While it may feel this way, in reality they are creating an atmosphere of mutuality where no decision is made unless they and those they are leading feel the decision is a good one. The teacher remains the leader and decides with students when it is appropriate to share in the decision making. Issues of safety are not compromised. When issues are negotiated, like the respect agreement, the group or an individual is far more willing to carry out the decisions that have been made.

The reality of using Option #1 most of the time is that the leader is only in the circle part of the time. Students spend a great deal of their energy figuring out how they can be in that circle. This creates power struggles. We have observed this paradox. More permissiveness occurs in Option #1 than in Option #4. A classroom example of this is students talking while the teacher (leader) is giving input. At this point the students who are talking are in the circle. The teacher continues to give input in spite of the talking, trying to reestablish his or her position in the circle—perhaps by speaking a little louder and more forcefully. A few more begin to talk because they notice others are talking. Because nothing is being done about it (in their minds), they figure they might as well talk, too. When there is too much noise, the teacher decides she or he must regain the circle. A common strategy is to choose someone and give him or her a detention. The talking subsides, but the person who has been chosen to set the example is very resentful. He or she may even loudly point out that it isn't fair because others were talking, too (they are now in the circle). The teacher might come back with a statement about life not being fair and that everyone better start listening or there will be more detentions (reclaiming the circle), and continue the lesson. Sometime it works and sometimes it doesn't. It is always very stressful for everyone.

In practice Option #4 is far less permissive and far more conducive to creating classroom communities where leadership is shared when appropriate, and therefore, there is no longer a need for power struggles. The situation above takes a much different direction. The teacher would observe that there is a conflict. The talking is blocking the time of giving input. Now those who are talking are invited into this problem-solving conversation. Perhaps they are talking to each other to get clarification about something that is being said. That time of clarification can occur and the lesson can continue. Or perhaps they are just chitchatting. Remembering the respect agreement, they may apologize and let the teacher know they will stop. Again, the lesson proceeds, but with a sense that it has been mutually agreed that all will listen.

Punishment

Some people feel there must be a punishment if a student does something wrong or violates a rule. The DTR structure does not call for punishment, and some see that as an obstacle. However, there are consequences for misbehavior or rule violations in this structure. Experience has taught us (Roxanne with very young adults, and Ron with college students) that it is a serious consequence to be called to make and keep agreements. Students with whom we have had several meetings, or who have had several meetings with each other, sometimes have to stop and think before agreeing to meet. The reason most often given for that is that they know they will be asked to think about making some changes, and then expected to do what they agree they will do. This is hard work and real accountability. Some even go so far as to say they would prefer a punishment because that seems easier and they don't have to make any changes. Punishment makes a person do something unpleasant but it is not accountability. After time to think, these students often come back ready to make agreements. Experience has taught them that simply refusing to meet for the purpose of working on the problem will not end the problem. The Flowchart maps the next steps, and they know that. The structure calls for involving more and more people in their lives to help get the problem solved. They learn that it will not just go away, and meeting brings resolution and help.

There is a whole field emerging called restorative justice. In retributive justice the questions are: What law or rule was violated? Who violated the law or rule? and What is the appropriate punishment for the one who violated the rule or law? Restorative justice asks different questions. Who violated the rule and who was hurt? What are the needs and obligations created by the offense? How can things be made as right as possible? How can the offense be prevented in the future? If you want to read more about restorative justice you may start by looking at some of the documents at peace. fresno.edu/rjp.

Teaching Students DTR Strategies When the Emphasis Is on Standards

Another reported obstacle is finding the time to teach students the strategies in the standard-driven environment of the public school. The DTR skills and strategies are embedded in the standards in several curriculum areas. Students are learning real-world problem-solving skills. They are learning critical thinking skills. They are invited to look at a process and then follow it step by step in a real-life situation. They get the chance to think creatively and to write what they think will solve the problem in a way that all can understand. They are invited to take responsibility for themselves and each other and to be leaders as they work on actual conflicts that affect their community. Utilizing the DTR Flowchart teaches standards in social studies, literature, math, and science. Students can also be invited to think in new directions in each of those subjects because of their training in conflict resolution.

For example, as students enjoy literature, their reflection about the conflicts that stories present can be expanded by inviting them to think of what different directions the story may have taken had the characters in conflict decided to use Option #1, #2, #3, or #4 to solve their conflict. They can think about how that would have affected the lives of the characters and whether or not the conclusion would have been different. They can then relate this back to themselves, their own conflicts and problems, and what might result based on how they decide to work at those problems.

History is another example that is often taught sequentially from one conflict event to another. Students can apply their learning related to conflict as normal and natural and see that it is important to have a variety of skills available in order to work on conflict because it will be present throughout their lives. They examine those conflict events, notice how they proceeded through the conflict cycle, and observe how these conflicts follow cycles that may start with confusion that leads to gathering injustices. We see how some proceed more quickly than others through the cycle of escalation that often leads to war (each side using #1). Once one side prevails, there is openness to other options such as consulting courts or use of the rule of law, and mediation/negotiation (putting #2, #3, and #4 to use). Students often observe how sad it is that we, through history, have not worked harder during the confusion stage using #3, #4, and even #2, and instead we move to #1 too quickly. They have the background concepts that enable them to envision what it might be like if we would stay in the mode of mediation/negotiation rather than moving so fast to force. The Flowchart and knowledge of it as a system seems to open the possibilities for some very deep thinking.

When DTR Is Not Practiced by the Whole School

Some may worry that following the DTR Flowchart is not something the entire school community will do. Even if your school community is not doing DTR, we believe just one person practicing it is a way to be a community change agent. When students are trained and excited about what they are doing, others will want to know about it. You can always figure out ways for them to have the experience, at least while they are with you. It is possible for you to follow the Flowchart as you relate to your students, and to have a special arrangement with your administrator or to develop a small "Thinkery" within your classroom. It is possible to mediate conflicts with your students and to encourage student/student mediation within your own classroom. Students begin taking on the task of spreading the news by using their skills at home and with other students informally and formally.

Teacher Preparation

The last reported obstacle we wish to address here is that of being prepared with the theory and the skills needed to put the structures and processes into practice. This book and the DTR Flowchart will help with that. The more thoroughly you read the strategies for understanding and the more you put them into practice, the more skilled you will become. If you have read this book, you are ready to start. The differences you experience as you practice will encourage you to keep practicing and improving. If you follow the Flowchart, you will find yourself moving from novice, to practitioner, to artist.

Any new skill takes practice, reflection, and more practice. Isn't that what we tell students? Teachers expect students to be willing to try new things and to practice them as they lead and guide them through the academic curriculum. As a novice, we encourage you to follow each of the steps of the Flowchart consciously. As you use them more and more, you will gain understanding, skills, strategies, and confidence. You will find yourself being a skilled practitioner. Occasionally you will experience an easy flow and remarkable results as the artist. It is important to remember to give yourself the privilege of being the novice at first and not expect yourself to be an artist immediately. We still find it exciting to improve at what we know to be good for students and for us, even if it is not our most natural, first response. As you gain experience using the Flowchart, you will find you have ideas for strategies that will improve the structures and processes as you practice and adjust to make them more comfortable for you and who you are. Students will add their ideas as well. That is what all teachers do with any curriculum. They use it, and mold it into something that is the most useful for their students and for themselves. You will be creating a social curriculum that will encourage your students to grow into more mature people who are independent enough to practice their individual freedom as well as to recognize and practice their community responsibility.

Concluding Thoughts

A goal of education is to help students develop into mature young people who are responsible and able to make good decisions. Educators want them to be ready and able to become positive participants and leaders in their families and communities. Educators must be teaching, developing and encouraging the skills each student will need in order to accomplish this. When these skills are specifically and deliberately taught and modeled, they will lead us toward realizing the vision of having restorative classrooms and schools.

Encouraging young people to be responsible for how they act in society is a gift to them and to the communities in which they will become active participants. Students often express how important is for them to be able to make positive contributions to the world around them.

The ability to meet one another in a problem-solving atmosphere and to talk about and create possibilities to solve conflicts is an ability that can be used on both the micro and the macro level. We view it as a very important part of the peacemaking work we are all responsible for doing in our world.

Works Consulted

Amstutz, Lorraine and Judy Mullet. 2005. *The Little Book of Restorative Discipline for Schools.* Intercourse, PA: Good Books

Augsburger, David. 1980. *Caring Enough to Confront.* Scottdale, PA: Herald Press

_____.1981. *Caring Enough To Forgive, Caring Enough To Not Forgive.* Scottdale: Hearld Press.

_____. 1982. *Caring Enough to Hear and Be Heard.* Ventura, CA: Regal Books

_____. 1992. *Conflict Mediation Across Cultures.* Louisville: Westminster/John Knox Press.

_____. 1996. *Helping People Forgive.* Louisville: Westminster John Knox Press.

_____. 2000. *The New Freedom of Forgiveness.* Chicago: Moody Press.

Bazemore, Gordon and Mara Schiff. 2005. *Juvenile Justice Reform and Restorative Justice: Building Theory and Policy From Practice.* Portland: William Publishing.

Bianchi, Herman. 1994. *Justice As Sanctuary.* Bloomington: Indian University Press.

Boers, Paul. 1992. *Justice that Heals.* Newton, KS: Faith and Life Press.

Braithwaite, John. 1989. *Crime, Shame and Reintegration.* Melbourne: Cambridge University Press.

Brueggemann, Walter. 1976. *Living Toward a Vision.* Philadelphia: United Church Press.

Bush, Robert A. and Joseph Folger. 1994. *The Promise of Mediation.* San Francisco: Jossey-Bass Publishers.

Canter, Lee and Marlene Canter. 2001. *Assertive Discipline.* Bloomington, IN: National Education Service.

Claassen, Ron. 1992. *Trust Building.* VORP Newsletter, March 1992. Fresno: VORP of the Central Valley, Inc.

_____. 2002. *A Peacemaking Model.* Fresno: Center for Peacemaking, Fresno Pacific University. available from http://www.fresno.edu/dept/pacs/docs/APeacemakingModel.pdf. Internet.

Claassen, Ron and Roxanne Claassen. 1987. *Making Things Right.* Fresno: Center for Peacemaking, Fresno Pacific University.

Claassen, Ron and Dalton Reimer. 2003 *"Basic Institute in Conflict Management and Mediation—A Manual"* Fresno: Center for Peacemaking, Fresno Pacific University.

Claassen, Ron, Charlotte Tilkes, Phil Kader, and Douglas Noll. *Restorative Justice: A Framework for Fresno.* Fresno: Center for Peacemaking, Fresno Pacific University.

Claassen, Roxanne. 2004. "School Discipline—Retributive or Restorative" (M.A. thesis, Fresno Pacific University.

Cline, Foster and Jim Faye. 2006. *Parenting with Love and Logic: Teaching Children Responsibility.* Colorado Springs: Nav Press.

Coles, Robert. 1998. *The Moral Intelligence of Children: How to Raise a Moral Child.* New York: Plume

Consedine, Jim. 1995. *Restorative Justice, Healing Effects of Crime.* Lyttelton, New Zealand: Ploughshares Publications.

Curwin, Richard and Allen Mendler. 2000. *Discipline with Dignity.* Upper Saddle River, NJ: Prentice Hall.

Dobson, James. 2006. *The New Dare to Discipline.* Wheaton, IL: Tyndale House Publishers

_____. 1992. *The Strong Willed Child.* Bonham, TX: Living Books.

Dreikurs, Rudolf and Loren Gray. 1990. *New Approach to Discipline: Logical Consequences.* New York: Dutton Adult

Fisher, Roger and William Ury. 1981. *Getting To Yes: Negotiating Agreement without Giving In.* New York: Penguin Books.

Fisher, Roger and Elizabeth Kopelman and Andrea Kupfer Schneider. 1994. *Beyond Machiavelli: Tools for Coping with Conflict.* Cambridge, MA

Fisher, Roger and Scott Brown. 1988. *Getting Together: Building Relationships as We Negotiate.* New York: Penguin Books.

Freire, Paulo and Myra Ramos. 2000. *Pedagogy of the Oppressed.* New York: Continuum International Publishing Group

Galaway, Burt, and Joe Hudson. eds. 1996. *Restorative Justice: International Perspectives.* Amsterdam: Kugler Publications.

Ginott, Hiam G. 1998. *Teacher and Child.* New York: Touchstone

Glasser, William. 1986. *Control Theory in the Classroom.* New York: Harper and Row.

Goleman, Daniel. 2005. *Emotional Intelligence: Why It Can Matter More than IQ.* New York: Bantam Books.

_____. 1998. *The Quality School.* New York: Harper Paperbacks

Gordon, Thomas. 1991. *Discipline That Works.* New York: Plume.

_____. 2000. *Parent Effectiveness Training.* New York: Three Rivers Press

_____. 2003. *Teacher Effectiveness Training.* New York: Three Rivers Press

Grey, Mary C. 2000. *The Outrageous Pursuit of Hope: Prophetic Dreams for the Twenty-first Century.* New York: The Crossroad Publishing Company.

Hocker, Joyce and Wilmont William. 1991. *Interpersonal Conflict.* Dubuque: Wm.C. Brown Publishers.

Johnson, Barry. 1996. *Polarity Management: Identifying and Managing Unsolvable Problems.* Amherst: HRD Press, Inc.

Kraybill, Donald B. 2003. *The Upside-Down Kingdom.* Scottdale: Herald Press

Kraybill, Ronald S. 1980. *Repairing the Breach.* Scottdale: Herald Press.

Kohn, Alfie. 2006. *Beyond Discipline: From Compliance to Community.* Alexandria, VA: Association for Supervision and Curriculum Development

Lederach, John Paul. 1995. *Preparing for Peace—Conflict Transformation Across Cultures.* Syracuse, NY: Syracuse University Press.

Lerner, Harriet. 1997. *The Dance of Anger.* New York: Harper & Row.

McElrea, Fred Hon. 1993. *Youth Court in New Zealand: A New Model of Justice.* Auckland, New Zealand: Legal Research Foundation, No. 34.

_____. 1994. "New Zealand Mode" chap 7. *Relational Justice.* Jonathan Burnside and Nicola Baker, eds. Winchester, England: Waterside Press.

_____, ed. 1995. *Rethinking Criminal Justice: Justice in the Community.* Auckland, New Zealand: Legal Research Foundation, Vol. I, May 1995

Nelsen, Jane. 2006. *Positive Discipline.* New York: Ballantine Books.

Northey, Wayne. 1994. *Restorative Justice: Rebirth of an Ancient Practice.* Akron: Mennonite Central Committee U. S. Office of Criminal Justice.

Peck, M. Scott. 1987. *The Different Drum.* New York: Simon & Schuster Inc.

_____. 1994. *A World Waiting to Be Born: Civility Rediscovered.* New York: Bantam Books.

Perry, John, ed. *Repairing Communities through Restorative Justice.* Lantham: American Correctional Association.

Pranis, Kay, Barry Stuart, and Mark Wedge. 2003 *Peacemaking Circles: From Crime to Community.* St. Paul: Living Justice Press

Schrock-Shenk, Carolyn and Lawrence Ressler, eds. 1999. *Making Peace with Conflict.* Scottdale: Herald Press.

Shawchuck, Norman. 1983. *How to Manage Conflict in the Church.* Leith, ND: Spiritual Growth Resources

Tavris, Carol. 1989. *Anger—The Misunderstood Emotion.* New York: Simon & Schuster.

Tutu, Desmond. 1999. *No Future without Forgiveness.* New York: Image Doubleday.

Umbreit, Mark. 1994. *Victim Meets Offender: The Impact of Restorative Justice and Mediation.* Monsey: Willow Tree Press Inc.

Ury, William. 1991. *Getting Past No: Negotiating with Difficult People.* New York: Bantam Books.

Ury, William, Jeanne Brett, and Stephen Goldberg. 1988. *Getting Disputes Resolved: Designing Systems to Cut the Costs of Conflict.* San Francisco Jossey-Bass Publishers.

Van Ness, Daniel W. 1986. *Crime and Its Victims.* Downers Grove: Inter Varsity Press.

Van Ness, Daniel W., Howard Zehr, and Kay Harris. 1985. *Justice: The Restorative Vision.* Elkhart: Mennonite Central Committee U.S. Office of Criminal Justice.

Van Ness, Daniel W., and Karen Heetderks Strong. 2002. *Restoring Justice.* Cincinnati: Anderson Publishing.

Volf, Mirsolav. 1996. *Exclusion and Embrace.* Nashville: Abingdon Press.

Worth, Dave. 1994. *Restorative Justice: Making Things Right.* Akron: Mennonite Central Committee U.S. videocassette.

Wink, Walter. 1998. *The Powers that Be.* New York: Doubleday.

_____. 1997. *When the Powers Fall: Reconciliation in the Healing of Nations.* Minneapolis: Fortress Press.

Wright, Martin. 1996. *Justice for Victims and Offenders: A Restorative Response to Crime.* Winchester: Waterside Press.

Zehr, Howard. 1990. *Changing Lenses: A New Focus For Crime and Justice.* Scottsdale: Herald Press.

_____. 2002. *The Little Book of Restorative Justice.* Intercourse, PA: Good Books.

The Authors

Roxanne Claassen M.A. is a teacher at Raisin City Elementary, a diverse K-8 school in rural Fresno County, California. She has twenty years of classroom experience at both the elementary and middle school levels. Roxanne has served as a mentor teacher, a beginning teacher support provider, and peer mediation coordinator. Roxanne and Ron co-authored a training book, *Making Things Right*, with 32 activities that teach conflict resolution and mediation skills. Roxanne has trained more than two hundred teachers to use *Discipline that Restores* in their classrooms and to initiate and administer student mediation programs in their schools. Roxanne honestly says that discipline is one of her favorite parts of teaching. Her Master's Degree in Conflict and Peacemaking enabled her to introduce and implement restorative discipline practices in her school. Roxanne uses cooperative structures and mediation to handle most discipline problems.

Ron Claassen M.A., M.Div., D.Min., is the co-founder (1990) and Director of the Center for Peacemaking and Conflict Studies at Fresno Pacific University. Ron teaches School Conflict and Mediation, Advanced Mediation, Restorative Justice, and several other courses in the M.A. Peacemaking and Conflict Studies Program at Fresno Pacific University. Ron also provides training, consultation, and intervention services in the community. The founder and former director (1982–1999) of the Fresno County Victim Offender Reconciliation Program (VORP), it was the first in California. He has extensive experience in both civil and criminal mediation and has trained thousands in restorative justice, conflict resolution, peacemaking and mediation. He is the author of numerous articles and training manuals including "Restorative Justice Fundamental Principles" adopted by the UN Working Party on Restorative Justice (1996) and *Making Things Right,* a curriculum for Schools co-authored with his wife, Roxanne. He was the recipient of the 2007 Carl and Esther Robinson Outstanding Advocate for the Common Good Award. In addition to consulting with many school districts Ron initiated and helped implement the Restorative Discipline policy at Fresno Pacific University.

11761799R00109

Made in the USA
San Bernardino, CA
29 May 2014